PENGUIN BOOK

Alone Across Australia

Jon Muir was born in 1961. At sixteen, after watching a documentary about Mt Everest, he decided to become a professional mountaineer. He climbed extensively in New Zealand and Europe before first visiting the Himalayas in 1982. He has taken part in five Everest expeditions, pioneering new routes and reaching the summit alone in 1988. He has also travelled thousands of kilometres by sea kayak, including a 52-day solo journey. The first Australian to have trekked to both Poles and climbed Everest, Jon was awarded the Order of Australia medal in 1989, the Australian Geographic Society's Adventurer of the Year medal in 2001, and the Centenary Medal in 2003.

www.jonmuir.com

Jon Muir

Alone across Australia

One man's trek
across a continent

PENGUIN BOOKS

Penguin Books

Published by the Penguin Group
Penguin Books Australia Ltd
250 Camberwell Road, Camberwell, Victoria 3124, Australia
Penguin Books Ltd
80 Strand, London WC2R 0RL, England
Penguin Putnam Inc.
375 Hudson Street, New York, New York 10014, USA
Penguin Books, a division of Pearson Canada
10 Alcorn Avenue, Toronto, Ontario, Canada M4V 3B2
Penguin Books (NZ) Ltd
Cnr Rosedale and Airborne Roads, Albany, Auckland, New Zealand
Penguin Books (South Africa) (Pty) Ltd
24 Sturdee Avenue, Rosebank, Johannesburg 2196, South Africa
Penguin Books India (P) Ltd
11, Community Centre, Panchsheel Park, New Delhi 110 017, India

First published by Penguin Books Australia Ltd 2003

1 3 5 7 9 10 8 6 4 2

Cover design by Debra Billson, Penguin Design Studio
Photography by Jon Muir except where otherwise attributed
Cover photograph of red desert sand © Australian Scenics
Maps by Damien Demaj
Typeset in 12/19 pt Horley Old Style MT Light by Post Pre-press Group, Brisbane
Printed and bound in Australia by McPherson's Printing Group, Maryborough, Victoria

National Library of Australia
Cataloguing-in-Publication data:

Muir, Jon, 1961– .
Alone across Australia: one man's trek across a continent.

ISBN 0 14 300126 4.

1. Muir, Jon, 1961– – Journeys – Australia. 2. Australia – Description and travel. I. Title.

919.4

www.penguin.com.au

CONTENTS

To Mary and Bob Muir, my parents,
for a lifetime of love, support and encouragement

ACKNOWLEDGEMENTS

I finally succeeded in completing the first unsupported traverse of Australia because many people, besides myself, believed the Great Mission was worth striving for.

Firstly, thanks to Brigitte for helping me in the realisation of my dream. Also to my family – Mum, Dad, Jim, my sister Pat, Peter and the little ones, Brianna, Beren and Arwenm – for their love throughout.

My principal sponsors for the mission were World Expeditions and the Australian Geographic Society. Without their help, I would never have been able to launch my repeated attempts.

For making the film a reality, I am especially thankful to Ian Darling and Shark Island Productions. Also to Martin Richmond and Sony.

Thanks to my minor sponsors, who, all up, provided massive help: to Fairydown for all the clothing that protected me from everything from snakes to storms; to Bogong for all sorts of odds and ends; to Freedom Foods for their sensational energy bars; to Bolle for sunglasses; to Outgear for my hauling harness; to Leki for my indispensable walking poles; and to Power Bar. A special thanks to Dave Mudie, Tim Wilkins, Synthetic Resins and RMIT for help with my various 'arid zone cruisers'.

There were many friends who drove me over to my start point at Port Augusta, or picked me up after my unsuccessful attempts: Peter Gray, Brigitte, Greg Pritchard, James Falla, Phil Wilkins and Nicky Sunderland.

Acknowledgements

Others helped me in preparing and procuring my equipment, another task I simply could not do all on my own: Jill McLeod, Peter Gray, Paul Deegan and Phil Wilkins.

The station owners I met along the way all provided me with encouragement and were happy to share with me their local knowledge. Thank you Malcolm and Colleen Mitchell, Stephen Lander, Bob Crombie and the boys from Adria Downs, Shirley and Howard Jukes, Colleen and Gordon McDonald, Hayley and Darcy Sutton, Emily and Ben Knight, Robin and Graeme Dale, and Keith Chapman.

My reception in Burketown was wonderful. Thanks to Sandy Hansen and the school kids, and to Craig Turnour, Chief Executive Officer of Bourke Shire Council. Also to Mal England, of Burketown Marine Charters, for taking me out to the open water of the Gulf of Carpentaria.

For helping turn my endless scrawls into this book, I thank Susan McLeish, Suzan Hobbs, Brigitte, and Ali Watts, who all played an important role in refining the manuscript. Thanks also to my literary agent, Selwa Anthony. And last but by no means least, thanks to Suzan Hobbs for helping me through the most difficult part of writing this book.

LIST OF MAPS

FOREWORD

The first thing that sprang to mind when I initially read Jon's journal was a very personal one: I was proud, yet humbled, to have been a part of whatever it was in his heart that led him to find his Holy Grail by walking across a continent.

Jon and I shared a lot over the years. There were times when we were close, times when we were far apart. Then last year, there was the time that saw us part ways. What remained had held us together for two decades and would see us through challenges ahead: a common passion for living life to the fullest.

I lived every day of Jon's great mission. In mid-May 2001, he and I drove two days from our hometown Natimuk in Western Victoria to Port Augusta in South Australia. I left Jon and his partner, our Jack Russell cross, Seraphine, at Yorkey Crossing, the limit of tidal salt water, with the promise that we would meet again in about six weeks' time at the top of Lake Eyre, Australia's biggest lake. By then, they would have walked a third of the way across Australia, on Jon's fourth attempt to cross the continent. The Great Mission – code name of his dream – was on again.

Jon is a very patient and methodical person. His dream as a sixteen year old was to climb Mount Everest. So in 1977 he dropped out of school, found a job, saved money and spent as much time as he could learning the art of climbing, in New Zealand, Europe and the Himalaya. Along the way he soloed the North Face of the Matterhorn, climbed new routes in the Himalaya and researched Everest, the mountains and the climbers.

In the years that followed his ascent of Everest in 1988, Jon decided to change direction and to ease off the intensive mountaineering and high-altitude climbing that had defined him as an outstanding achiever in the wilderness. From the top of Everest he had gazed at the brown Tibetan Plateau and reflected on how much it reminded him of Australia's own arid landscape. This started a thought process and a new dream which later defined itself as the urge to take a long journey, unsupported, through the most arid and lonely parts of the Australian continent.

Back at home, Jon immersed himself in countless books about Aboriginal and European pioneers, about the landscape and moods of the country he wanted to cross on foot and, most importantly, about Australian wild food resources. This thorough apprenticeship sprinkled with trials and errors in the field took over a decade and brought a finely tuned Jon to the 'Great Mission – take four'.

The meticulous preparation paid off. Jon walked 2500 kilometres from Port Augusta in South Australia to Burketown in Queensland in a style he describes as 'unassisted', carrying with him everything he would need for the traverse, and supplementing his rations with hunting and gathering along the way. He used roads and other vehicle tracks as little as possible, and only crossed one bitumen road in the course of his four-month odyssey.

Jon chose his route after much reflection. Taking the shortest route across the continent made sense: after all, no one had ever tried to achieve what he set out to do. The two options were from either Spencer Gulf or the head of the Great Australian Bight, to the Gulf of Carpenteria. The latter route meant negotiating the Great Victoria Desert and its hundreds of east-west dunes with a fully loaded cart. It simply did not add up. Spencer Gulf to the Gulf of Carpentaria it had to be. Within this overall line, Jon chose a route that stayed away from civilisation as much as possible. It also meant that he would be cutting right through the centre of the driest part of the Australian continent.

Doing a new route involves a lot of detective work. Had early pioneers followed his planned route? No, they had not, although he would cross the path of a number of them on his chosen line. What about the Aboriginal people? Had any of them crossed the whole continent? Unlikely, but who knows – adventurous spirits are not a product of today's society alone! For years Jon researched his route and its potential downfalls and resources with the care and dedication he gives anything dear to his heart.

Finding information on the route was one thing, coming up with the right equipment for the job another. Jon developed and built an 'Arid Zone Cruiser', a wheeled cart made especially to deal with the conditions he anticipated on his trip. Amongst the bits and pieces collected and adapted for the journey, was a homemade distiller, which desalinated water well enough, but did nothing to improve the taste of the resulting broth. On his little cart he also packed a DVD Cam, a solar panel, sleeping gear and clothing, as well as staple foods: rice, flour and muesli, olive oil, a little chocolate and breakfast bars. At the start of the trip, the total weight of his food was around 46 kilograms. He supplemented this as he went along. For safety reasons, Jon also carried an emergency satellite beacon, or EPIRB

Last but not least, he invited along one dog – our two-year-old Jack Russell cross, Seraphine Snupesen. She was supposed to be my dog but I went away guiding in South America for a month when she was still a puppy and when I came back, *she* was wife number one. Seraphine went on a fully catered walk across Australia, and as long as she was with Jon, following scents, digging rabbits out of holes and running, she didn't really care what he was up to!

The first three attempts had gone over my head really. The landscape in which they took place was all too different from what I was used to. I had not heard the beat of Australia's deepest heart yet, but I was to feel it that winter of 2001. There is a big map of Australia on the wall at Hope, the paradise retreat we had bought in the Grampians. Each time I was there, I touched the place I last heard Jon had been at, and I sent him on, with all my heart, always further in the great unknown, mental and physical.

I told Jon at the start of Take Four that he would make it, and if I had many stomach cramps during the journey, I never had a doubt. He did, and these appear at dramatic times in his amazing journal. For a good reason; the Great Mission was by far the hardest challenge he had ever contemplated. A new route to the South Pole? That was easy compared to this, he told me at the end of the crossing. He added that every single day he marched on the mission was harder than his summit day on Everest. This says a lot: Jon carried a 23-kilogram pack to the summit, alone, without fixed ropes or guides, Sherpas or Westerners, and battled his way up in snow sometimes up to his waist. That gives you an idea. Let me tell you, not many people do it that way.

And so, after thirteen years of preparation and four attempts, the Great Mission dream became a reality, and one well worth sharing with others. After reading Jon's journal I felt a duty to help him tell his amazing story. A duty, what am I saying? An honour, a pleasure, a learning experience. I became the initial editor, losing myself in Jon's journal and travelling again with him, this time through words, across Australia's incredible landscapes. It took a lot of time, energy and heart-ache for me as our circumstances changed to see this book to completion.

This book is the result of our getting together on an incredible project. When the feelings were behind the words, I helped to pull them to the surface. When I did not understand, I asked questions. *Alone Across Australia* is an amazing journey through our continent home, and into the deepest corners of the human soul.

I hope you enjoy the experience and learn as much as I did.

Brigitte Muir, 2003

THE
BEGINNING

I hugged Brigitte. 'Be safe,' she said, 'and have fun. I'll see you in a couple of months on the Warburton Creek.' She gave Seraphine, our Jack Russell cross, a last tickle on the belly and then she was in the car, closing the door, driving off with a smile full of tears. Feeling a bit numb, I made my way back to the camp I had established the day before. It was very empty suddenly. Our last night together had been a strange one: I already gone in my head, not daring to let my fences down, she treading carefully.

The next day I was to start on my fourth attempt to cross the continent of Australia without support from anyone. Me, walking, all the way from the tidal reaches north of Port Augusta in South Australia to a distant Burketown up in northern Queensland, was this how I really wanted to spend the next four months? I looked at the horizon to the north. Twenty kilometres away I could see the twin summits of Nacoona Hill. I pictured the country beyond, the land I knew so well from my previous attempts – the massiveness of Lake Torrens, and the Gibber Plains and desert country. Then beyond that, the table-lands, the tropics and the Gulf of Carpentaria. So far. So long. So hard.

Yes, it was exactly where I wanted to be. To be about to embrace the challenges that this beautiful but rugged country had in store. To revisit some of the land I had come to love, and then to push beyond that land into the unknown. That exhila-rating unknown, exciting but also daunting. I had prepared myself physically, and mentally readied myself the best I could for the attempt, but the size of the challenge before me made me feel small, weak and vulnerable. Could I do it?

On 28 May 1988, I summited Everest on my own. Finally, after thirteen years, I had achieved my boyhood dream. Sitting on the summit, with no more steps to take, I wondered briefly, what next? As I looked around me from the apex of space, the brown, rolling hills of the Tibetan Plateau caught my eye and reminded me of Australia's barren interior, a place I had never visited but one I'd flown over often on my way to the Himalaya or the European Alps.

As a child I spent all my spare time out in the bush. Exploring, adventuring and making spears, bows and arrows, claypots and cubbyhouses. The bush was where I was happi-est and where I felt I belonged. Perhaps the time had come to act on a long-harboured desire to learn something of survival in my own country. I was a living paradox, really: my climbing experience meant I could survive in some of the highest, harshest landscapes of the planet, in places so extreme that humans can only visit briefly, but plonk me down in the dry expanses of my own country and I'd have little idea how to survive! And yet the Aboriginal people have made a living there for 60 000 years.

Sitting in front of a map and dreaming of journeys has always been a favourite pastime of mine, and the next time I did it I let my eyes wander over Australia. The challenge that leapt out at me took my breath away – an unsupported traverse of the continent. Unsupported – no assistance from pack animals or vehicles, no pre-laid depots, no re-supplies, relying entirely on my own energy. I was sure that nothing like it had ever been done, and wondered whether it was even possible. Well, there was only one way to find out. But before I could even think of setting off, I had a long road to travel to gain the skills and knowledge needed for survival. I had done it with Everest, gaining experience from the day I first touched ice at sixteen to the moment I stood on top, eleven years later. I could do it again.

As often happens in life, events overtook me. My wife, Brigitte, was at that time attempting to climb the highest mountain on each continent, the so-called 'Seven Summits'. I joined her for the third summit, Aconcagua in Argentina. She had summitted the normal route on her own, and now it was my turn. I made a one-day ascent and then joined Brigitte and our friend Geoff Little at base camp, before the three of us moved on to attempt Aconcagua's extremely difficult 3000 metre south face. It turned into an epic struggle for survival that we barely managed to win. We had been to hell and back and I promised myself never again to take on such a dangerous objective.

During the early nineties Brigitte and I started an international guiding business, but my Australian mission was always at the back of my mind.

No one had ever attempted an unsupported traverse of Australia. Why? Had it crossed anyone's mind to try? The amount of knowledge required for such an adventure means years of study and experience of the different ecosystems encountered on a continental traverse. No one seemed to have all the facts or the answers to my questions. C. Warren Bonython had pioneered the idea of unsupported traverses of deserts in the 1970s, when he and Charles McCubbin crossed the Simpson Desert with only one re-supply. But these were relatively short trips, and I was looking at a much longer one!

From 1990 to 1995, during holidays and time off I found myself drawn to my own backyard. I studied bush food and survival techniques from specialist books and explorers' accounts, but more important than that, I then set out to the bush to practise. I made quite a few trips of up to three weeks each during this period, surviving solely on bush food for up to two weeks at a time. These trips, during which I turned information I had gathered from books into personal experience, were vital and, as I suspected, just as challenging as any of my mountaineering expeditions. Just like safely climbing a mountain, living off the land requires a high level of commitment, judgement and knowledge. Many changing factors must be constantly taken into consideration, with the understanding that decisions made will not only influence a successful outcome but also survival itself.

Amongst other things I learned what was edible and what was poisonous, how to extract water from plants in an emergency situation, how to conserve water, and techniques for reducing the time it takes to gather tiny fruits.

To successfully traverse the continent I also needed to understand her weather and her terrain. This information I gathered from studying weather patterns and rainfall charts over many years, and poring over maps and first-hand accounts of the land.

During this time I also returned twice to Everest, the last summit in Brigitte's quest. I wanted to be her climbing partner. These expeditions were all I needed to confirm that my heart lay in the empty regions of my own country, far from the crowds, fanfare and nonsense that inevitably accompany a climb of the world's highest peak.

Now that I was beginning to understand what this trip required, my mind turned to making it possible. In waterless country you need to carry at least four litres of water a day to survive, and the only way to carry enough for a decent-length journey is to haul it along behind you. An effective 'cruiser' would be the key piece of equipment in making the 'Great Mission' – code name for my planned traverse of the continent – possible. The cruiser would need to be large enough and strong enough to carry my loads of equipment, including guns, clothes, shelter tarps, sleeping gear, food rations and water containers – everything I would need to be totally self-sufficient for up to five months – but manoeuvrable and light enough for one man to pull it some 2500 kilometres!

So, in 1996 I built my first arid zone cruiser. The 'Super Cruiser' was a cart built from timber wrapped in Kevlar (an extremely strong material much like fibre glass) and heavy All Terrain Vehicle (ATV) wheels. It consisted of a simple timber frame with two wheels, about one metre apart, and two shafts that come up the front of the frame and clip into the waistband on the pack-harness. I now needed to test both the cruiser and my ability to move across the desert with a massive load. I chose the Lake Eyre region for a trial run, and in the winter of 1996 headed out on the 'Walk to Nowhere' with 260 kilograms of water, equipment and food – enough for forty days.

The walk was pure magic – extremely tough but unspeak-ably rewarding. I covered 620 kilometres, unsupported, of the driest region of Australia. The only people I saw while I was out there were two scientists who were busy, heads down, dig-ging a hole in the sands of the lake's foredune. The first they saw of me were my feet, in sandals, less than a metre away from them. I was dirty, dishevelled and unshaven, and I think I scared them no end!

Towards the end of my wanderings I sat on the top of a massive sand dune in the Tirari Desert, of which I had just done the first unsupported traverse since Aboriginal occupation and looked around. The walk to nowhere had been the most physically demanding expedition I had ever undertaken. Hauling everything I needed for a prolonged trip in desert country had taken me closer to my physical limits than anything I'd attempted before. At the end of most days I found myself far more worn out than the day I'd broken trail through deep snow to reach the summit of Everest alone. I was under no illusion that an unsupported crossing of the continent would make all my previous expeditions seem like training trips. And yet, I felt at home in this arid country – it was time to attempt the Great Mission. I would have to wait until the following winter though, as walking across the whole continent without being re-supplied is only possible in the cooler months. Summer temperatures in the deserts can reach 60°C (140°F), and in that heat you can't carry the volume of water your body needs to survive. Also, my equipment needed fine-tuning. The Super Cruiser had worked well on the Walk to Nowhere, but at 29 kilograms it was too heavy for a longer journey. The next one I built had large moulded Kevlar wheels that reduced its weight by 10 kilograms.

Take one. The route I had carefully chosen, was one that allowed for the quickest traverse combined with water sources not more than 200 kilometres apart and reasonably flat going. All of this meant I would be cutting right through the centre of the driest part of Australia, and staying away from civilisation as much as possible. I was to walk from Mystery Island (just north of Port Augusta), in the middle of a claypan that marks the limit of the tidal reach of the Spencer Gulf, to Burketown on the north coast. A trip that I estimated would take me between three and four months.

Peter Grey dropped me at Mystery Island, in mid-June 1997. Ideally it should have been mid-May, but I'd been waiting for Brigitte to return from her successful Everest climb, and what with being personal assistant to her and fine-tuning my gear, I was a month late. Ahead of me stretched the 2500 kilometres to Burketown, on the Gulf of Carpentaria. Such a great distance with a massive load – it was a daunting thought. I started slowly but steadily, which went well. But after just one week my Kevlar wheels began to disintegrate and I had no choice but to give up. I walked 50 kilometres to the closest road and hitched a ride to the Port Augusta bus station.

Back home, I decided to launch another attempt immediately. I replaced the Kevlar wheels with the original ATV wheels, losing my weight advantage but gaining strength. The winter was now well advanced and I realised there would be no chance of reaching Burketown if I was delayed even a little. As it was I would be marching in the tropics in late spring; any later was out of the question. So, Brigitte and our friend Greg Pritchard drove me back to my starting point and once more I headed north. No luck this time, either. I was stopped by drought-breaking rains after going 200 kilometres without a problem. It poured down for a week, and with no end in sight

I was forced to accept that my hopes and dreams had once again come to nothing.

I took it in my stride, but my motivation and energy needed another outlet and Brigitte blessed my decision to head to tropical Queensland. I travelled the 800 kilometres separating Cooktown from the tip of Cape York, alone, in my sea kayak – no mean feat for someone who is scared of water! It took 52 days and I lived almost entirely off the land and sea.

The next two years saw me concentrating on an old dream of walking to the South Pole. I had been invited by Eric Philips to join his 1998–1999 expedition and simply couldn't refuse. Eric wanted a three-person team and I recommended Peter Hillary. Peter and I had spent a lot of time together climbing on Everest in the 1980s. The trip was a disaster, for although we were successful in pioneering a new route to the Pole via the untrodden Shackleton Glacier, the combination of personalities was a nightmare. Oh well, if nothing else it was good training for the Great Mission!

My third attempt had to wait until the next winter I was available, that of 2000. This time I didn't set off alone. Seraphine, the Jack Russell cross, although originally Brigitte's dog, had fallen in love with me and I with her. I had never travelled with a dog before and invited her along – she could attempt a fully catered traverse of Australia. I had a new cruiser built with the help of Lachlan Thompson and the team at the Royal Melbourne Institute of Technology, but once again, 200 kilometres into the trip, I had wheel problems. One of the bearings fell apart and sent me back to the Port Augusta bus station and the drawing board.

Was I losing faith? Not really, I never expected this massive challenge to be a walkover. Though a very optimistic person, I'm also a realist. I take whatever happens in my stride and see my repeated failures as valuable lessons along the way. What I was attempting was a giant leap beyond anything that had been achieved in unsupported desert journeys, and only by getting out and giving it a go could I learn what would and would not work. It's always the question mark that interests me. The bigger the question mark, the better. The Great Mission was the biggest question mark I'd ever faced and I was determined to give it my best shot. It was increasingly obvious that to have any chance of success I must get absolutely everything right – make the right decisions, carry the right equipment – and even then I had to rely on the weather and the country to play the game. In my previous three attempts, equipment failures and weather conditions had prevented me from giving the mission my all. I needed another go at it.

On returning home I took a long, hard look at the various carts I had trialled. I chose the best features of each to build two new cruisers, the 'Tirari Twins'. They were smaller than the Super Cruisers and used a type of ride-on mower wheel. Time to do some field testing.

Brigitte, Seraphine and I headed out for a family holiday in the Tirari Desert. We were hoping to do the first longitudinal traverse of this desert (my second traverse of it) – the Tirari was starting to feel like a second home to me. Over the next two weeks we crossed its 200 kilometres from south to north, and except for too many punctures the carts performed well. Prickles are vicious in Australian deserts, but by placing a 4-millimetre strip of greenhide between the inner tube and the tyre, I was able to get rid of the problem. I was confident that the last hurdle had been overcome. All I needed to do now was get out my well-read lists of gear and food, and make coats and leather boots for Seraphine.

So, on 14 May 2001, Brigitte the driver, Seraphine the team member and I the expedition leader left home for the fourth attempt at the Great Mission, with a car full of food and equipment. Was it going to be fourth time lucky?

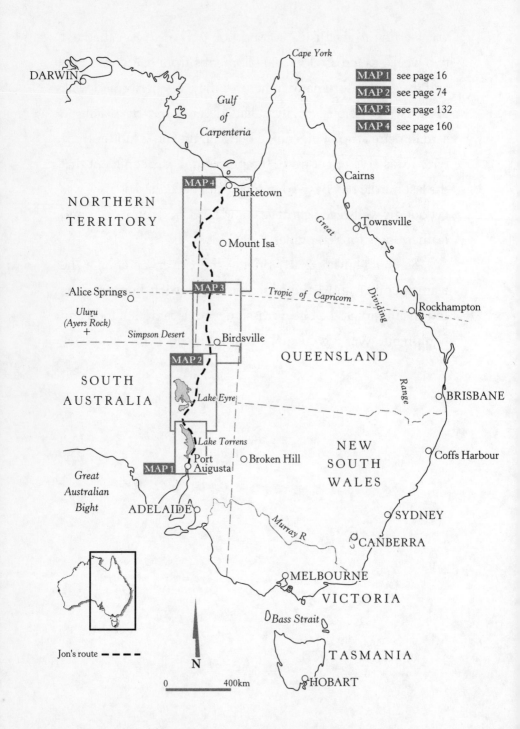

MAP 1 see page 16
MAP 2 see page 74
MAP 3 see page 132
MAP 4 see page 160

DARWIN

Cape York

Gulf
of
Carpenteria

NORTHERN
TERRITORY

MAP 4

Burketown

Cairns

Townsville

○ Mount Isa

-Alice Springs-

MAP 3

Tropic of Capricorn

Great

Rockhampton

Uluṛu
(Ayers Rock)
+

Simpson Desert

Birdsville

QUEENSLAND

Dividing

SOUTH
AUSTRALIA

MAP 2

Lake Eyre

Range

BRISBANE

Lake Torrens

NEW
SOUTH
WALES

Coffs Harbour

Great
Australian
Bight

MAP 1

Port
Augusta

○ Broken Hill

ADELAIDE ○

Murray R

SYDNEY

CANBERRA

MELBOURNE

VICTORIA

Jon's route ━ ━ ━

Bass Strait

N

TASMANIA

0   400km

HOBART

OVERVIEW OF JON'S ROUTE

THE
JOURNEY

Salt Ck

Termination Hill +

Andamooka

Depot Ck

Nankabunyana Ck

Mount Deception +

Leigh Creek

SOUTH

AUSTRALIA

Gaiger Bluff

Warrioota

Creek

Lake Torrens

Nilpena Ck

Woomera

Parachilna

Andamooka Ranges

Etowie Ck

St Mary Peak +

Wilpena

Flinders Ranges

Wilpena Pound

Poison Bore

Mount Eyre +

Beda Hill +

Willochra

Ck

0   25km

Hawker

N

Nacoona Hill +

Mystery Island

Quorn

Emeroo Range

Map 1

Legend

○ Town
□ Homestead/Station
● Waterhole/Bore
+ Mountain/Hill
⎯ Road
⁓ River/Creek
- - - Dingo Fence
▪▪▪ State Border
▨ Lake/Gulf

Port Augusta

Spencer Gulf

Jon's route ▪▪▪▪

MAP 1: MYSTERY ISLAND TO LAKE TORRENS

1

MYSTERY ISLAND TO LAKE TORRENS

Starting Out

DAY 2: THURSDAY, 17 MAY
Mystery Island, 10 km north of Port Augusta

Here I am again: Mystery Island, the start of my traverse of the continent. Mystery Island is a clay and sand hill in the middle of a 5-kilometre-long claypan that marks the limit of the tidal reach of Spencer Gulf. Where its name comes from, I have no idea, though for me it seems fitting. I have camped here with friends on three of my four attempts at the Great Mission, and always the feelings are the same: excitement, trepidation, doubt. The beginning and the end of great journeys are times of intense emotion and awareness, with so many questions about myself and the land that only the future can answer. A mystery.

Ahead of me this time is the awesome challenge of travelling on foot from the waters of the Southern Ocean on the south coast of Australia, to the tropical seas of the north – a

17

journey of about 2500 kilometres – without support. This means no resupplies of food or equipment, no help from pack animals or humans, and very little human contact along the way. I am facing an extreme solo adventure.

It was hard for me to farewell my love this morning. Although we have planned one meeting en route, on the War-burton Creek in seven or eight weeks time, it seems harder to part each time as the years roll on. Now that I'm alone sud-denly, I find myself in a slightly melancholy, contemplative mood. In the weeks and months ahead there will be times when I am striving not simply to complete the journey, but struggling for survival itself – am I strong enough in body and mind? The melancholy should mostly clear when I get going, but for the moment I'm stuck here by rain showers that are making the route ahead impossible.

I went for a wander after returning from walking Brigitte back to the car, and found something amazing – the lower jaw of a wombat was sticking out of the eroded mesa on the north side of the island. It must be ancient as I know wombats don't inhabit this part of Australia today. I want to photograph it and film it – do a little David Attenborough number. It will give me practice at filming and take my mind off the enormity of the task ahead.

On this walk I am carrying a video camera and all the paraphernalia that goes with it. It all adds up to a lot of extra weight, but I am determined to make a documentary of my attempt at the mission. I want to share my experience with a wider audience. I hope it will inspire people with a message of how simple life can be. All too often in our headlong rush into the computerised world of the twenty-first century we lose sight of the animal within us all. The animal, like all others, that doesn't need much more than water, food, shelter and social interaction.

It's later in the evening now and I just took a walk out on the claypan. Claypans are dead-flat, low-lying areas common in arid Australia. This one is a bit different to most, as it is occasionally inundated by the sea. Its surface is littered with seashells and I picked up several and pocketed them. I'll carry them across the continent and return them to the sea on the north coast. Perhaps they will bring me luck.

DAY 3: FRIDAY, 18 MAY
Mystery Island

It poured down on and off all last night. There is now a pool of water between the tarpaulin, which will be my only shelter on this walk, and the place where the tent Brigitte and I shared was pitched. The ground is heavy although a windy day with lots of sun has dried it considerably, and I am not sure about leaving tomorrow. The weather is still unsettled, with lots of cloud to the east and west of me. My fingers are crossed for no more rain but

I am staying on top of things mentally, which is the main thing. These long, extreme journeys are as much a journey of the mind and spirit as the body. It would be all too easy for this delay to allow negative thoughts to creep in. Great things are achieved with a positive attitude, a negative one will always fall short.

On the positive side, I collected 12 litres of water from the tarp during the showers. I have designed the tarp specifically for this purpose, with many tie-off points to which I can attach my ski stocks to prop it up and make a catchment area, or bottles of water to weigh it down when I have collected enough. It can be quickly rearranged to maximise either rain collection or protection if the wind shifts. There is no problem with food, either. I still have a few days' supply from the car journey here, so I haven't started on my rations. Still, it is mildly frustrating after all the excitement of the departure from home to be stuck here! I must view this as a false start rather than a setback. My true beginning will be when I march north from here.

This afternoon I climbed the sandhill to the north-east that Brigitte and I climbed in 1997 at the start of my second attempt. The years fly by with incredible speed and I really hope this is my last time on Mystery Island. That this time, finally, the mission will be completed. Starts are always hard.

I must relax. Today is only my first day out here and I must try not to dwell too much on all I have left behind, but to look forward to all that lies before me. I am very pleased to have my faithful little dog, Seraphine Snupesen, with me. She is almost two years old and though small in stature, thinks

20

she is a lion. Before we left, friends asked whether she would be able to keep up with me. The truth is that she has the energy of ten men, and if I could keep up with her this journey would take two months rather than four!

7 p.m. Dark clouds and a little spitting rain; time to do a bit of reading. I brought along a book by the Belgian adventurer Alain Hubert. It is the journal of his crossing of Antarctica and sounds like the escape I need.

DAY 4: SATURDAY, 19 MAY
Mystery Island

This morning I woke up to a beautiful sunny day with a light wind. I went for an exploratory walk early on, but the ground is still too wet for marching. I would get nowhere pulling a cruiser in these conditions: the wheels would get coated with sticky clay-mud, which stops them turning in no time at all. The ground surface should be okay by tomorrow, so I used my time today to finish work on Seraphine's boots although she won't need them just yet. I bought her a pair of leather, laced booties specifically designed for working farm dogs, but the ones I purchased were too big for Seraphine, so I have had to modify them to fit her tiny paws. Also I sorted myself out generally for the start of the walk.

So tomorrow I begin in earnest on the greatest challenge of my short life. My previous journeys in arid Australia and my first three attempts at this walk have left me in no doubt that travelling 2500 kilometres on foot across mostly desert country and pulling everything I need, will be more demanding than anything I have accomplished before.

Some elements of this expedition will be similar to other international trips of mine. On long unsupported walks, the weight of everything one needs is far too great to carry on one's back, so it must be hauled along behind. In Antarctica this is on a sled; here in Australia it is on a wheeled cart. In Antarctica, however, the terrain is far easier to negotiate. There, one travels for weeks on end over flat snow with the only obstacles being sastrugi, wind eroded lumps of snow usually less than half a metre high. Crossing Australia I will haul over hundreds of sand ridges up to 20 metres high, and cross thousands of dry water-courses, many up to 15 metres deep and requiring tortuous climbs into and out of them. There will be areas of dense vege-tation to battle through and areas covered by large rocks, not to mention rivers, swamps, salt lakes – all hauling a massive load of up to 150 kilograms – day after day, week after week, month after month.

Mountaineering, for the most part, is comparatively 'cushy'. The majority of time on a climbing expedition is spent lounging around resting. Of course, these times are interspersed with days of extreme physical work but they tend to be the exception rather than the norm.

I hope the gods are kind – I need them on my side. My body must remain strong and healthy, with no injuries, my mind must keep positive, focussed and balanced, the weather can't stray too far from the averages (too much rain and I can't move, no rain and there may not be enough water for survival), and my equipment must not break down.

Before she left, Brigitte gave me a box of chocolates with each chocolate wrapped in a message. There is one for each week of my trip. They were already a bit squashed and melting and the ink was running on several of the messages so I had to undo them all and store the messages in an envelope. I even managed not to read any in the process – but I ate all the chocolates!

DAY 5: SUNDAY, 20 MAY
foot of Nacoona Hill, Nacoona

Now I've really started. I did 15 kilometres in 4 hours – a solid beginning. Last year I found a much easier route over this first section than I had used on my first two attempts, and this time I even managed to improve slightly on that. On the eastern side of the dry salt creek that runs into the Mystery Island clay-pan is a series of reasonably open clay flats that offer relatively fast travel. Here and there were low ridges of yellow sand that for the most part I was able to avoid.

I find new beauty in the vistas slowly opening at every

step I take. Even at this early stage I am starting to see the beauty in the detail of this country. The ripples in the sand on the side of the dunes swim before me and just like them I am weaving an erratic course across the continent. Everything I pass on the way has its own unique beauty, from the spirals on a dead leaf to the magnificent craggy peaks of the Flinders Ranges to my east.

So the walk went well and I managed a reasonable pace without difficulty, but I had a hard last half-hour. There is no point in pushing things at this point. My body and mind need to ease into the mission, so I have taken the rest of the afternoon off. Well, not really *off*: I broke the camera tripod head this morning, which needed fixing. While I looked for a suitable piece of wood to carve as a head replacement, my thoughts wandered back to the march.

I've broken this massive project down into stages of approximately 200 kilometres each, based on the changing geographical features I plan to traverse. Stage One runs from tidal salt water (Mystery Island) to the toe of Lake Torrens; Stage Two is 200 kilometres up to the east shore of Lake Torrens; Stage Three crosses the stony gibber plains to the Tirari Desert; Stage Four crosses the Tirari Desert itself; Stage Five follows Warburton Creek; Stage Six, the Eyre Creek; Stage Seven, the Mulligan River; Stage Eight crosses the Mulligan River and heads for the Georgina River; Stage Nine follows the Georgina River; Stage Ten crosses the Barkly Tableland; Stage Eleven follows the O'Shanassy River; and Stage Twelve, the Gregory River.

Although these stages make it sound like I'll be following watercourses for much of the journey, in fact most of them rarely flow and I am expecting the going to be arid and tough. My pace will depend on the particular stage I am on but generally I'd like to average 20 kilometres per day. I imagine I will have individual targets for each day, but this will be wholly dependent on the conditions I encounter and more importantly, the condition of my body!

The kilometres per day will also increase as my load is lightened, which will happen two ways – gradually, as my rations are consumed, and in spurts, as I leave equipment at various points along the route. As I will be travelling north, with the temperature increasing, I'll be able to ditch some of my cold-weather gear and also various bits and pieces of equipment, such as one of my two lightweight sleeping bags and maps, that I can do without for the sake of speed and distance. None of it will be lost, however, as Brigitte and I will drive back this way and pick up any caches that I leave behind. It will be fascinating to be going in reverse – backwards along my route and taking on weight instead of shedding it!

Apart from the stages, the other thing that will break my journey a little is the few times I come into human contact. This will be firstly with Brigitte at the Warburton Creek, and then after the Arunta (Simpson Desert) at several remote cattle stations. These visits are mostly to make contact with Mission Control, to give them my position, but also to gather valuable information about local terrain and conditions.

The final, vital, part of my plan is my summit push. This will happen near the end of my journey, when I reach a point where I have little remaining food and equipment. Then I will abandon the cruiser and strike out for the gulf with just my hauling-harness-cum-pack. I hope to be able to move quicker over this last stretch, as carrying a pack is faster than hauling; also I could never negotiate parts of the north country with the cruiser. It's all an enormous weight to move, considering the distance I've got to travel, even without the unpredictable variables. My mind also seeks out comforting familiarity – what would Brigitte be up to on this Sunday afternoon? Probably reading the weekend papers on the back verandah.

So, one step at a time. The tripod repair will be a bit of a saga requiring several afternoon sessions I should think. The thread holding the head to the centre strut has snapped off. It will not be an easy job. I am camped at the base of a beautiful dune covered in casuarina trees. They whistle and sigh in the light breeze as I work on the tripod. The weather is fine so I won't put the tarp up. That means one less thing to do in the morning, which will make for a quicker getaway.

On long desert journeys, my day always begins with the sound of the alarm clock in the dark. Sometimes I have my usual breakfast of muesli in bed, then I brush my teeth before packing everything on the cruiser. The last thing I pack is the sleeping bag because Seraphine likes to sleep in. She sleeps curled up in the bottom of my sleeping bag, sometimes poking her head out to watch me pack the camp up and load the cruiser. She is always reluctant to climb out when it is time to go. As soon as it is light enough to see, I am off to make the most of the cool early mornings. It can be cold around dawn so as I break camp, I often wear my jumper, woollen fingerless gloves and sometimes my lightweight down jacket, then strip down just before leaving. It doesn't take long to warm up; pulling the cruiser is hard work. On the march I wear my walking boots with gaiters to keep dust and prickles out. The gaiters are also good for snake protection. I also wear long pants, a long-sleeved shirt, a scarf and a hat for sun protection. Around my neck I carry my map in a waterproof map case, a compass and my watch. The watch has been on every expedition I've made over the past 12 years, and is like a trusted partner. I would consider it bad karma to lose it, though I do carry a spare just in case.

Which route will I take tomorrow? Should I go around the hill for a change instead of over the pass as on my previous three attempts? I will sleep on it. Sunset is at 5.20 p.m. or so and as I only have limited power for my head torch, it's early to bed as usual.

DAY 6: MONDAY, 21 MAY
between Nacoona Hill and Lake Torrens

What a struggle! I decided to go up and over the pass and though I am now sure that it is a better route than going around Nacoona Hill, it was still desperate. I gained 100 metres in the space of 2 kilometres, most of it in short rises of loose sand. Despite taking it very slowly, sweat poured off me, soaking my shirt and stinging my eyes. What else should I expect? The cart, equipment, food and water weigh over 150 kilograms – a heavy load when the terrain is flat, let alone on a slope.

The 'arid zone cruiser' weighs only 19 kilograms on its own and consists of a simple timber frame with two wide, all-terrain vehicle wheels about a metre apart, and two shafts that come up the front of the frame and clip into the waistband on my pack-harness. The 'deck' of the cruiser, however, is stacked high with the massive amount of equipment I need. This includes water containers, guns, maps, clothing, shelter-tarps, sleeping gear, a repair kit, first aid stuff, film gear, and dozens of other bits and pieces, not to mention 45 kilograms of dried food, including 6 kilograms of dog food! To help propel myself as I haul along, I carry a ski stock in each hand.

I get swamped by mental lows at times, but generally keep a handle on them. The first days of big solo journeys are always like this for me. Until I get in a groove, until I get the whole machine going like clockwork, there is uncertainty, there is doubt . . . Why am I out here? Why am I alone? The answers will soon be clear once more, but for the moment it is hard to chase the demons away. I try to forget about Burketown but it's no good. The mammoth distance plays on my mind as I toil and sweat along, today at only 2 to 4 kilometres per hour.

Behind it all lies the question, as yet without an answer: Can I do it? This will be my last attempt unless something other than me claps out in these first weeks. But I believe that this time the equipment is right for the job, and I hope the outcome does hinge on me – my strength, stamina, experience and will. If I am not up to the challenge, I shall accept defeat with grace. Having to give up due to equipment failure once more would be almost too much to bear.

I strolled along a nearby sand dune in the evening stillness. Seraphine is always more relaxed at the end of the day and together we enjoy these special times. Moving around without having to haul the cruiser gives me a sense of weightlessness. Not having to think about the best route virtually every step of the way frees the mind, enabling it to wander more easily. The light is soft and magical at this time of day, and this evening the Flinders Ranges positively glow red and purple, floating like a hallucination above deepening shadows.

These moments make me remember why I am here and why I love being on my own. I come for the beauty that surrounds me in the natural world and the inner peace that flows through me when I immerse myself in it. Alone I experience this more clearly and more intensely. There are some of my earlier questions answered.

DAY 7: TUESDAY, 22 MAY
somewhere

I am struggling to do 15 kilometres per day and thought it would be easier than this, but I am trying not to worry. It's a long journey and I must get into it slowly. My muscles need time to adjust to the regime of hauling and it is here at the start that I am most vulnerable to a tendon, ligament or muscle injury. I remember Borge Ousland, the most experienced polar traveller on the planet, saying he went out too hard at the start of his first attempt at an Antarctic traverse, gave himself injuries and wore himself out. I must avoid this, but even after just four hours in the harness I am feeling it. The terrain is so much more demanding and unpredictable than that of the Antarctic, where one can march for weeks on end across a flat, unchanging icescape. Here the landscape is constantly changing, with deep, steep-sided dry watercourses to climb in and out of, sand dunes to struggle over, dense vegetation to push through . . . Every muscle in my body is being taxed to its limits and I've only just begun!

That's okay, my body will soon remember. Bringing Alain Hubert's book was a really good idea. He is a very experienced expeditioner and reinforces what I already know I must do, both mentally and physically. It is good to read about someone else's struggle, even if just to remind myself that I am not alone in my obsession with attempting the seemingly impossible.

The cruiser is going well but is a bitch in the loose sand of bare dune crests. The weight on it is too great for the wheels' width and the tyres sink into the sand. I must try deflating them a bit and see if that helps. I have been pushing on my stocks so hard I have blisters on my palms. And on my precious feet? Only one small one on a toe so far. Fingers crossed I can keep it to one. It's my feet that will carry me across the continent and I must pay particular attention to them. Despite wearing gaiters it's impossible to keep all the fine particles of grit out of my boots. Every evening I shake out my socks and wipe between my toes hoping to help prevent the onset of blisters. Also, my new boots are great, the most comfortable ones I have ever worn.

I settled down to what I expect will be my standard dinner during the mission: a tiny amount of rice with some local bush tucker. I will be making the most I can of the bush tucker along the way. For me this will consist mainly of meat, greens and fruit. There are carbos to be found on the land too, but they take an extraordinarily long time to gather and prepare and I just don't have the time. Therefore, on the cruiser are over 40 kilograms of rice, flour, muesli, energy bars and chocolate, which I'll be supplementing with native fruits, vegetables and meat. The more successful I am at hunting and gathering, the longer I can stay out here, which increases my chances of completing the mission. I try to use as little of my carbohydrate stores as possible each day.

Today I shot a rabbit and also gathered some pigweed, a succulent green vegetable, so I'll be going to bed with a satisfied stomach. I also gathered some nitre-bush berries, which taste like salty grapes, that I will add to my muesli in the morning.

I just realised that today is Day 7. Yippee, time for a chocolate message!

'I love you, that's it. Be safe and never doubt.'

Just what I needed to hear.

The messages were a good idea.

DAY 8: WEDNESDAY, 23 MAY
nowhere again

Nowhere in particular, but tomorrow I will reach the toe of Lake Torrens, or its near vicinity, and the first, though admittedly the smallest, stage will be over. A minor milestone and thankfully the official end of the start.

I took it a bit easier today. Well, that's how it mostly felt, yet I walked 1 kilometre more in the same time as yesterday. My body is remembering. My mind is also slowly relaxing and this should continue as the days go by and my confidence grows. Well, hopefully. This terrain is so difficult, with many small dunes scattered all over, in whose loose sandy crests the cruiser takes on weight because of the drag. If you think walking in soft sand on beach dunes is hard work, try it pulling 150 kilograms! Thankfully, there are a few solid claypans where the going is good, and I definitely move faster on these smooth-bottomed flat areas.

I knew what was in store, of course. I have been here on

a previous attempt or two, but maybe, just maybe, I can find a better route this time. Brigitte's words have given me strength and courage. 'Never doubt.' It played around in my head a lot today, and helped me to see that so far it has been a good start: slow but very steady, with no major hiccups and my mind is beginning to relish the daily struggle and challenge.

Wilpena Pound came into view occasionally today and this set me thinking about the stormy, wild night Brigitte and I had together on the highest summit of the Flinders Ranges. Wilpena Pound is a sandy plain covered in a forest of native pine and surrounded by a ring of spectacular, jagged rocky peaks. We ascended St Mary Peak, the highest of them, in torrential rain driven by gale-force winds. In the afternoon the rain turned to snow, which is rare in this arid desert country. Miraculously it cleared briefly to reveal one of the most beautiful sunsets I've ever had the good fortune to witness.

I finished fixing the tripod today. The head is now glued in and cannot swivel – oh well. I also had to take out the central shaft bolt of the cruiser as the nut was rubbing on the tyre. The last thing I want is a wear spot and a puncture.

DAY 9: THURSDAY, 24 MAY
Willochra Creek

I've camped here before, on this small terrace near the crest of a massive sand dune overlooking the intermittent salty pools of Willochra Creek. That was in 1997, on my second attempt. Four years ago – a lifetime! What also seemed like a lifetime was today's 4.25-hour struggle to cover just 11 kilometres as the crow flies. Still, I recovered quickly and now, not long after stopping, I feel fine. I think I'm just about ready to start marching 5 hours a day.

My heart stopped beating earlier on: one of the wheel bearings is making a noise. A possible looming disaster. The noise has been around from the start of the trip, but I thought it was due to the central shaft bolt rubbing on one of the tyres. Yesterday I took the bolt off, but the noise remains. It doesn't sound *too* bad, but it is of huge concern. If these lightweight aluminium axles die soon I'll have to get the steel axles sent to me. This would constitute massive assistance though, and I feel that if that were needed, it would be better to give up and try again next year. I hope and pray it doesn't happen. I am not ready to give up my mission just yet. There's nothing for it but to press on.

I am in dunes and flats country. Some of the flats are fantastic – open, smooth and hard – while others require a fair bit of route-finding around vegetation. The dunes are hell, though.

I am now level with the southern end of Lake Torrens, which is about 5 kilometres west and just visible from where I am camped. Stage One is over! My mantra for the time being: be patient, relax, don't push too hard, accept what comes your way, and enjoy the little happenings of the walk.

I went hunting once I established camp and caught a rabbit. My gun is a single shot .22 rifle, so there is no second chance if I miss. Also I have a .303 for larger game. It takes a lot of time and patience to get close enough for a sure shot, but there is no greater motivation than hunger. As I write my journal, I am keeping an eye on my rabbit, roasting over coals on a skewer. Yum.

2

LAKE TORRENS

Lost in Mirage

DAY 10: FRIDAY, 25 MAY
near Poison Bore

Desperate, desperate, desperate! I had a good start but then I entered a dune system which was not marked on the map. There was no time to psych for it and I had to cross lots of the bastards. My cruising speed went down to 1 kilometre per hour and I was working possibly harder than ever in my life, slowed to a crawl by the heavy sand tugging at my wheels. Many times today I was forced to stop in my tracks, not for a planned rest, as one takes doing any sustained activity, but because I couldn't take another step, period. This is as physically extreme as it gets. I'm spent for now. All I can do is head for Lake Torrens, which is 5 kilometres away, and hope for a better route.

This latest challenge has made me incredibly motivated though, so if this body, this equipment and this dog can hold together, there is still a chance. To complete the dream would be well worth every torment along the way.

Despite the difficulties, I am enjoying the struggle, step by step. Each step itself must be careful and well placed, to maximise the energy and to minimise the risk of injury. And of course the movements of the cruiser must also be brought into the equation. In any given scenario I know exactly what it will do, from experience. For example, if the left wheel hits a rock, plant, log, anything, then the harness will tug at my hip and I must heave my left shoulder forward to get the wheel over. After a while the machine sort of becomes part of you: the beast of burden and the burden are one! The harness I use was designed by Eric Philips, with whom I trekked to the South Pole, and me. The two shafts of the cruiser clip into the waistband, one on each side. The shoulder straps also connect directly into the shafts, and everything is adjustable, allowing me to loosen the waist and haul more through the shoulders, and vice versa.

As the day ends, I find myself in the middle of a large pine forest, native of course. It is hard to see more than a few hundred metres from the dune crest, because it is so dense. From a particularly high dune I climbed earlier I could see all around. In the fore- and middle-ground there was nothing but forest and sky, and in the distance the Flinders and Andamooka ranges.

I'm now due west of Mount Eyre. It was renamed after the explorer Edward John Eyre, who came this way in 1840 and followed the Flinders Ranges north, utilising their permanent waterholes. These water sources made him optimistic of traversing the continent. However, when Eyre reached the end of the range and climbed the northernmost summit, all he could see were giant salt lakes to the west, north and east, barring further progress. He called the mountain Mount Hopeless. It was to be another 21 years before Burke and Wills made the first traverse of Australia.

I also got a few glimpses of Lake Torrens today. Just a fraction of its massive brown expanse peeking between the dunes on the horizon to my west. Soon it will become a big part of my life.

Large black clouds moved over my camp at sunset and are trying to rain. The tarp is up, ready to catch precious water.

DAY 11: SATURDAY, 26 MAY
still near Poison Bore

The rain woke me with a thousand thundering pricks on the tarp, filling my nostrils with a rich, damp odour that is rare in this desert country. It does mean another day's delay though.

I've filled up my 20-litre plastic water container plus a few others. As I lie in bed enjoying a forced rest, with Seraphine snuggling at the bottom of my sleeping bag, I wonder what Brigitte is up to this morning. My mind reaches out to her, I miss her, I love her. Are you at Hope with your girlfriends? Alone like me? Or in Natimuk visiting friends? I cannot know.

I'm making the most of this day off by taking it easy. Well, sort of. There are always a few jobs to do, and today's might include transferring some more food from the main supply bag to the more accessible weekly one; doing a bit of sewing; and with all the water I've collected, washing myself and some clothes. Then I must sharpen my knives and put sticky tape to mark water levels on the 20-litre container, as the texta marks are fading.

Despite my chores it is wonderful to lie down and bask in the simple pleasure of doing nothing but absorbing my situation passively through my senses. Really I should take Seraphine for a walk; it would be good for both of us to stretch our legs. She seems to enjoy this forced halt as much as I do.

The day is turning out to be not so bad. There is a good wind with a mostly sunny sky (25 per cent cloud cover) and I hope to hit the road tomorrow.

It's now late afternoon and I am reading a bit and writing a bit. Blast! Black clouds move in again . . .

DAY 12: SUNDAY, 27 MAY
Lake Torrens

Brigitte's Everest summit day! It is four years ago today that she completed her seven summits quest by reaching the top of

Everest, on her fourth attempt. I celebrated the anniversary with an extra Fisherman's Friend on a dune overlooking Lake Torrens.

I feel smaller and less significant as the days go by and that feels good. The lake ahead merges with the sky. Looking to my west now, there are a few mountains, including Beda Hill, I think it is, which looks like Uluru (Ayers Rock), and the hills of the Andamooka Ranges.

Extricating myself from the forest this morning took me south-west of where I started. South – back towards Port Augusta! It could have been demoralising but instead I decided to enjoy the forest and it worked a treat.

When I finally reached Lake Torrens I had a good run along the lakeshore. The edge is slightly wet, which is almost certainly a good thing: the light, dry, fluffy and flaky dust is a no-go. So at present things are looking good and maybe I'll start to move along more quickly. It has to happen sometime.

And another thing, I ticked over my first 100 kilometres today. About bloody time!

DAY 13: MONDAY, 28 MAY
Lake Torrens

My Everest summit day! Thirteen years ago today, I stood alone on the summit of the world's highest peak and looked out over the vast brown Tibetan Plateau. Now, here, I have another big, brown, empty space to captivate my imagination. I love these giant salt lakes. Their vast, desiccated and sterile nature lends them a purity that is unique. Only in Antarctica have I experienced something similar.

All I have seen of Torrens so far is brown – a rich earthy brown that stretches to the horizon where it merges with the sky in a perfect curved line. Not like the blinding white salt sheets of Eyre, Gairdner or Frome, the three other massive lakes in this region. Just brown. Many walks on these lakes over the years have given me a deep love of the subtle play of light across their surfaces, and I look forward to getting to know Torrens better in the days ahead.

I should have made the most of my earliest getaway so far but a morning rainbow was too beautiful. I stopped to admire its delicate beauty and to film it. The good run along the shore continued for 3 kilometres or so, then the ground became too wet from the shower forming the rainbow. Damn! So I came back away from the shore and the going was difficult and slow with lots of weaving, and bumps and bushes that are unavoidable. I was so keen to do better today that I upped the hours. In fact I probably would have done this anyway as I felt strong in the harness.

I glimpsed the tops of what must be some quite spectacular small islands very close to the lake's edge and from where I am now camped I have a great view of the Flinders Ranges.

Seraphine is going along well and I guess I am too. She covers at least twice the distance that I do in a day. In the mornings in particular she is ranging all over the place, sniffing here, scratching there, darting off after a bunny, but rarely straying more than 50 metres from me. We keep an eye on each other. Sometimes a particularly interesting smell will sidetrack her and she will fall behind awhile, only to come bounding up from behind a few minutes later, overflowing with joy and excitement. It is a beautiful experience to travel with her on this mission. She is so full of life and enthusiasm for the walk itself that some of it rubs off on me, and given that I'm not short of this myself, there is an abundance. Our bond grows stronger by the day and I do worry about my puppy in the wilderness. Dingoes or foxes could kill and eat her, Wedge-tailed eagles could carry her away, a snake could bite her – it's a big world for a little dog!

I think, breathe and plot WATER: my ultimate obsession. How much is left, how much am I drinking, how fast am I going, where will I next get some? It would be hard not to be constantly asking myself these questions: I've got three days worth of water at the moment. It's not something I worry over, I just keep it to the fore of my mind. I could have collected some today as it seems most of the creeks entering the lake have pools of salty water, but I don't want to end up carrying much more than I need. It slows me down and wears me out. Finding the right balance between carrying too much and carrying too little requires having a handle on lots of variables. I draw heavily on my experience to get it right, and I must get it right constantly, or the game will be over. Like I said, it's an obsession.

Tomorrow is Day 14 – little note from Brigitte day!

This evening I did something I had been thinking about for a while but hadn't had the courage to do. I got out the next map, mid-Torrens to the start of the Tirari Desert, and lay it down above the current one. It was a shock to see how little distance I've come, and that's just looking at the bottom two of my twelve conglomerate maps!

However, features are appearing on the horizon that were not visible yesterday. Seeing a mountain shimmering in a mirage a long way off to the north, across the easternmost section of the lake, helped reassure me that I am actually getting somewhere. From the map it turns out to be Mount Deception. Last year my cruiser packed it in a day or two after sighting Mount Deception. Better not do the same this year!

DAY 14: TUESDAY, 29 MAY
Etowie Creek, Lake Torrens

'Can you hear the ocean? Let's hit the beach when you are done with Australian sands!'

I probably could have heard the ocean from here once upon a time, but not any more. It's now 150 kilometres in one direction and 2000 kilometres in the other. Add to that the fact that my hearing is not so good and, no, I can't hear the ocean. But it's funny, just today I thought back to our last time at the beach together, not long before I came here. So I guess in another way I *can* hear the ocean. And yes, let's go to the beach on my return. Yippee!

Today's march was very similar to yesterday's, sometimes on the lake, sometimes on or in behind the foredune. Slow and laborious. I'm starting to sound like a broken record! Still, I am now marching 6 hours a day and feeling better for it than the 4 hours a day I was walking when I started. The problem is not enough daylight hours. I'm busy from before first light till after dark, with very little – if any – slack time. It's amazing how long it takes to do everything by yourself.

Each day after my march, I try to find a campsite that has good shelter from prevailing winds and that isn't overrun with insects. The ideal site is near food producing plants, a rabbit warren, water of any description, firewood, and has a good view! If it looks remotely like there is possibility of rain or morning dew, then I erect the tarp. Often I position the cruiser in such a way that I am able to use it as one of the four main tie-off points for my shelter. The rest are tied out to bushes and shrubs near ground level and my ski poles are used to prop the tarp up in the centre. I then take my sleeping bag, mat and big kitbag off the cruiser and organise my bed and dinner. In the kitbag are all the things I need to access on a regular basis – up to a week's worth of my staple foods, head torch, cooking gear, maps, journal, camera equipment and clothing. It also contains Seraphine's food and water containers, which I take out first so she can have her dinner when she pleases. I also usually put on her home-made rabbit skin coat at this time.

Next I collect just enough wood to cook dinner with then write up my log and journal and mark the days march and campsite on my map. Though I have my overall route across the continent carefully planned, I must constantly study my maps to try and pick the best day-to-day route.

Most evenings I do small repairs or modifications to my equipment or a little filming. There may be fruits or green vegetables nearby that I gather, and there is always the possibility of a hunt at any moment so my gun is always handy. After siphoning out 4 litres of water from my main 20-litre container into my two 2-litre bottles, I get on with lighting the fire and cooking dinner. When all this is done I've just about had it, so turn in ready to wake up to the sound of my alarm and begin the next day!

I am due west of Wilpena Pound now, so of course times with my love are at the forefront of my mind because I can see a landmark that bonds us. It is great to share journeys and holidays with others, to join in the laughs and banter around the fire at night and to be able to get different ideas on the best plan of action or a fresh outlook on a difficulty or problem. When I am alone there is none of this, and I must be a one-man team. But on the other hand, my relationship with the land is incredibly intense when I am alone. My humanity has no point of reference and so I'm able to merge more easily with the land. Alone I am at my strongest, my best. No energy is spent interacting with another person and I can focus more fully on the challenge at hand.

Despite being not too far from road and rail it is quite remote down here on the boundary of the Lake Torrens National Park. It would be a real surprise to see someone. There's simply nothing going on down here. It is wonderful.

DAY 15: WEDNESDAY, 30 MAY
Lake Torrens

Today was my 10th day on the move. It was also the third of my new 6-hour-a-day marching regime. I am now feeling quite strong physically but the terrain is so tortuous it is impossible to establish a rhythm, except when I am on the lake. The lake has generally been a bit soft and heavy and the mud sticks to my wheels, but where possible I follow it, as the alternative, the shore and its environs, is more difficult.

As I've always known, Lake Torrens, the second stage, is proving extremely difficult and I am progressing very slowly at just 15 kilometres per day as the crow flies. I accept it and I keep going. From my previous attempts and walks on and about the other salt lakes, I am under no illusion about the rugged country that borders them. There's no point getting negative about it; I know things will be quicker in the Tirari Desert where the terrain is easier and I am familiar with it. It should also be faster on the stage following that one, along the Warburton Creek, where I won't have to carry much water as it is flowing at the moment. As for the stage directly after this one, I'm pretty sure the gibber plains from the top of Lake Torrens to the Tirari will also be fast, but I'll just have to wait and see.

I do get amazing views as I struggle along, with the rugged Flinders to my right, and this massive lake and its mysteries to my left. Mirages play across the surface of the lake all day long. Islands are lifted off the surface and can 'float' above the flat horizon, hanging in the sky for hours at a time. On one of my previous salt-lake journeys, I witnessed the extraordinary sight of my two companions, about a kilometre from me, turned upside down and walking along in the sky on their heads. On another occasion, alone on Lake Eyre, I had been heading for the north shore some 70 kilometres away across the flat, feature-less surface of the lake. Looking up after checking my compass, I stared incredulously at what had suddenly appeared. The fore-dune of the north shore had been lifted and brought forward so that it stood in perfect detail apparently just 1.5 kilometres dis-tant. After re-checking my compass to make sure I hadn't made a mistake, I watched it start to bend and waver before vanishing as suddenly as it had appeared. You can't always believe your eyes in these magic places.

Back to the mission at hand. Mount Deception has taken form and is no longer a fairy castle in the mirage. It will be a solid landmark for many days to come. The peaks of Wilpena Pound, 50 kilometres to my east, are especially impressive with their rocky spurs and ridges, their tangle of summits. This is as close as I'll be to them. From here on the mountains can only get smaller and it will be a sad time when finally they slip from view altogether.

DAY 16: THURSDAY, 31 MAY
Lake Torrens

Well, more of the same. The immediate environs of the lake's edge have become a bit more contorted so I have moved away from it a little. Bit by bit, things get better – the load is getting lighter and I am becoming stronger and more efficient. The pace has also increased, and my average now is 17.2 kilometres per day if I exclude days off. In my original plan I was supposed to average 18 from the start to Muloorina Station, so I am on target to at least achieve that. Optimistically I hope it will be closer to 20 kilometres a day or more, as I am sure I will speed up on leaving the lake.

It is getting dark now, and the weather, which has been building towards a storm all day, is looking like it might just deliver. I'll take what comes. To top up with rainwater would be great; distilled water tastes horrible and is a pain to produce. The way I get it is by filling my homemade pressure cooker-cum-distiller with salty water, then I sit it on a roaring fire. Soon enough, steam goes through the plastic tube attached to its top, into the copper coil cooling in a bucket of water, and presto, condensed drops fill my waiting container. Pity it does not have a peaty, malty taste!

Of course, if it does rain I'll be in for a further day's delay. I guess I'm lucky to be able to see the positive side first. But it is more than just 'seeing' the positive; it must be believed in and followed with one's heart and soul.

I was reorganising my food and found a couple of cups worth of coffee from Mystery Island. A treat! I don't drink coffee or tea as they are diuretics and I can't afford to lose liquid as soon as I drink it. I'll save them for the Warburton Creek though. That way I can enjoy a cup with my love; we have arranged to meet in early July. The plan is that I will call her from Muloorina Station on the south side of the Tirari Desert and give her an estimated time of arrival on the north side, at Warburton Creek. As I have crossed the Tirari twice before, I should be able to guesstimate this reasonably accurately. Brigitte will only come if she can bring along a friend or two to witness that I am not resupplied in any way.

Hey, I just realised I have only got one pen with me . . .

DAY 17: FRIDAY, 1 JUNE
Lake Torrens

Today has been a good day, and for a number of reasons an important one. Often I had clear views from dune crests and several things I could see gave me a good idea of how far I'd come. In the south, fast fading into obscurity, is the Emeroo Range, where I began. Not only does it look far, but it *feels* far.

To the north, Mount Deception has turned from a dark blob into a mountain with spurs and ridges, and a low range to its south-west has appeared. Past both of them to the north, Termination Hill has put in its first appearance. I've passed the northernmost point of my previous three attempts, and clicked over 200 kilometres. Psychologically it has all come together to give me a big boost. Maybe I can do it! But then maybe I should just forget about that and concentrate on the walk I am on now, the length of Lake Torrens. Regardless of my progress, I have become more relaxed and am enjoying things more, even the marching! My body is feeling stronger too, and maybe soon I'll add another hour to my daily march, which currently stands at 6 hours.

The route today was the best since arriving at the lake. I marched 2 to 4 kilometres from the shore in the region where the dunes to my east peter out. This is not always nicely defined, of course, and I did have to cross some dunes, but overall the going has been good. For the first time I hit some decent-sized, hard, flat areas that enabled me, at least for a while, to get out of first gear.

This is the nicest camp site I've had for a while. It is located at the base of a long and beautiful dune that is higher than most and nicely vegetated, with open sand on the crests punctuated by the odd tree or stand. The views from the top of the dune are perhaps the best I have had so far this trip. The moon is more than half full now and as the weather appears to have settled I am sleeping out tonight. Well sort of – I'll lie under some low branches to keep the dew off, should there be one.

DAY 18: SATURDAY, 2 JUNE
Nilpena Creek, Lake Torrens

Big day out and I am tired. The terrain today made things difficult. Hummocky and sandy with lots of vegetation – what a contrast to yesterday.

Not long after starting, I passed close by a huge active rabbit warren. I kept going until I was out of sight of it, then tied Seraphine to the cruiser before backtracking with the gun. I found a good firing position and lay down quietly in the dirt. About 10 minutes later, out came a bunny. Bang! I remained motionless for another 10 minutes. Bang! Two rabbits for my tuckerbag today. After hunting we wasted a lot of time in the tangle of the Nilpena Creek and its many branches. I am camped on one now, and in the morning I think I'll head straight for the lake and try my luck there.

Tomorrow I will be moving on to a new map. The landscape has swallowed me up and I have simply become part of it. I am no longer feeling like an outsider, like something that doesn't belong. I am a minuscule part of the environment – a part that has a place, like ants, bees, grubs, leaves and rocks. I just can't get the words right. My thoughts are clear but communicating them properly sometimes seems beyond me.

Anyway, it's a beautiful place to camp, this creek bed. I found an old well nearby, with an ancient tank beside it and a few sheets of iron, an old pot, and signs of a simple tin structure a few hundred metres away. A track goes by it. The water, 15 feet down, is salty. I reached it by placing a rock in one of my nylon stuff sacks and tying a long cord to it. Was there ever fresh water in the well? I can only assume there was, given the ruin nearby. Who stopped here? Where had they come from? Are they now buried somewhere nearby? Everywhere I go has a thousand stories to tell, but no one to tell them. I am alone.

DAY 19: SUNDAY, 3 JUNE
Warrioota Creek, Lake Torrens

This has been a day of mixed blessings, which, all things considered, has been fun. Seraphine and I marched down to the lake shore first up, which was terrible at that point, so we settled for the country just in behind the foredune. Sometimes good clay, mostly terrible humpy sand, this terrain is just about the slowest it gets.

Seraphine was having some problems with the prickles today, and stopping often to get them out. She is now quite adept at this compared with her first desert walk, and having marched several hundred kilometres (at least), her paws have toughened up. Nevertheless, she was causing too much delay, so I put her boots on. Initially she was very clumsy in them and appeared self-conscious, a situation not helped by my hysterical laughter. Soon she forgot them, however, and it was business as usual.

Late in the day the nature of the lake's edge changed so I gave it a go. Not bad – a little soft but much better than anything else that was on offer. As I approached Warrioota Creek, the surface of the lake became too thickly vegetated to travel on. Never before have I seen so much growth on a big salt lake. It is only a foot high but too dense to move through, and in places it extends out on the lake surface for I don't know how many kilometres – at least three, probably more.

I am now camped in the dry bed of the Warrioota Creek. It has several main channels but is a floodout area, meaning there are also many smaller channels. There is a line of gums along each of the two main channels.

I am facing a water crisis over the next while. Nothing drastic of course, but I may have to stop for a day soon to desalinate a batch of water. Perhaps I'll do that tonight if I can find a salty pool around here.

Over the next 30 kilometres there are three creeks that I *think* will have water. (Well, that included this one!) After that there is not a single creek for a while. In fact, in the 90 kilometres between Depot Creek and the lake's north shore there will be just one source: Mulgaria Watercourse. Mind you, I'm not holding my breath on that one as on my map it doesn't even rate the dubious title of 'creek'. So, I could be in for a bit of a dry stretch and I would feel more confident starting with water already desalinated, rather than doing it on the trot which is not quite as efficient. I'll sleep on it.

What I am facing next is the top section of the lake, the remotest part of it. North of here a dune field to the east makes escape problematic. I'd briefly considered heading out to the east at this point, avoiding the dune field and getting myself into slightly better watered country than here by the lake. But although following the lake's edge over the next 100 kilometres will be more difficult than heading east, I don't want to have to leave Torrens because the lake route is more remote, with no fences or vehicle tracks. It is the end of the farmed world and the beginning of the glorious no-man's-land of the lake. I'll stick with Lake Torrens.

These tough decisions do remind me that to successfully complete this walk, I've got to get everything right every time. I must find and carry enough water to keep me hydrated, hunt and gather plenty of food to supplement my stores of carbohydrate and so enable me to stay out for four months. My body needs to be well looked after and remain injury free. My mind must remain alert and focused and my equipment cared for and maintained

DAY 20: MONDAY, 4 JUNE
Lake Torrens

A funny sort of a day. First up I spent all morning looking for water. I left the cruiser at the camp site, taking just the hauling harness with my two collapsible 20-litre water containers strapped to it, as well as my digging trowel and rifle, and set off up the dry bed of the Warrioota Creek. It is lined with beautiful tall gums, and I was confident of finding a small pool of water. The creek itself is in a deep gutter with steep earth banks 5 metres high. In places, large gums grow out of the middle of the creek bed and at the base of these are deep holes where water remains after floodwaters subside. Today, though, they were bone dry and the further I travelled, the more despondent I became. After a few hours I gave up and returned to camp, having wasted the morning in a fruitless search that covered 18 kilometres and wasted valuable water. I then thought I'd better march some distance towards Nankabunyana Creek, so as to be able to reach it tomorrow. It drains the whole of Mount Deception, so I am reasonably confident I'll find salty pools at its mouth – fingers crossed.

During the afternoon a storm has been building and I have seen showers to the south-west over the lake, so this could also get me off the hook! I am disappointed to have wasted the morning and only marched half a day, but there is nothing I can do about that except learn from the experience.

The reward for my big day is light rain tonight, and I have collected 2.5 litres of water from the tarp.

DAY 21: TUESDAY, 5 JUNE
Nankabunyana Creek, Lake Torrens

What an amazing day it has been and still is! The plod up Torrens continued on past Gaiger Bluff to the Creek. Gaiger Bluff is an ancient-looking, eroded and crumbling cliff of soft yellow rock. I climbed to its summit and gazed out across the vast, empty, timeless landscape. I feel smaller with each passing day. My insignificance is highlighted by my isolation. After a time travelling alone across the landscape it is easy to believe I am the only person on the planet. The world beyond the mission has now completely fallen from my shoulders and I rarely even think about it.

From Gaiger Bluff, I could see a great open dune face on the north side of Nankabunyana Creek and was optimistic of finding water. But on arrival, what had looked like a tiny pool turned out to be salt glistening on top of the clay.

The light was odd today with a storm increasingly likely as I made camp, and I crossed my fingers for rain. I couldn't rely on that, however, and decided to go about finding some water to desalinate. I dug a hole and found water, but it was very bad quality, full of salt and lots of minerals. It clogged the desalinator pot very quickly, and the water also seeped into the hole so slowly that it took me an hour to fish out 5 or 6 litres. Despite this, I got the fire revved, the distiller on and away she went. Meanwhile the storm kept building, and I could feel it about to happen. Nevertheless, I continued with the still and in 50 minutes I had desalinated 1 litre. When the second litre was done the rain began. The tarp was already up and waiting, and I had also laid out my second tarp, this one on the ground. As thunder, lightning and rain began I lay out all my clothes on the second tarp for a sky laundromat session, shuffling between filling containers and standing naked before the flames. The rain and the heat invigorated me enormously and I laughed out loud at the simple beauty of the situation, while Seraphine cowered under the tarp.

It took 2 hours to fill everything but the wine bladder, about 60 litres in total. I put the ski pole back in the centre of the tarp, pushing its centre up to give myself more room under it and to shed rain evenly. It looks like I will be here a few days. Still, I'll get to go hunting and have time for a good rest. Perhaps I can dry some more meat. Seraphine and I both love it, and it is a very simple process: I slice the meat in long, thin strips that I simply hang over a nearby dead tree. The sun and the wind do the rest.

A lot of rain has fallen and continues to – for 3 hours now it has been coming down and it still seems like magic to us.

'I look forward to an Australian adventure with you.
A challenge for both of us.'

DAY 22: WEDNESDAY, 6 JUNE
Nankabunyana Creek, Lake Torrens

Well it rained all night and on and off this morning. There are many pools of water about and Lake Torrens looks like an inland sea! Of course, with all this water about I'm wondering how much to set off with. I'll take a few walks around and monitor what is going on before I leave, but I am confident that for a few days at least I'll be collecting water from these rains. Perhaps this storm is a blessing after all, allowing me to complete the length of the lake without carrying much water.

On and around the foredune area the terrain tends to be mostly sandy, which means it drains quite fast, and it may not be long after the rains end that I can make a start. Obviously the sooner I get going the better – at present it is hard to imagine doing the whole walk in anything less than 120 days. Will I be a skeleton by then?

Has it been a quiet day off? Ha! I have been a busy little beaver and done lots. The weather cleared after lunch to a perfect sky but now dark clouds are moving in from the northwest. Could it be more rain? I don't need any more, thank you very much! Again I am wondering how much of what I collected I should carry. Most of the claypans are drying quickly. To check just how quickly, I am keeping track of the dropping water level of a number of them. I will check them again in the morning before I leave, unless too much more rain falls. This will help me decide how much to haul when I go. Another minor advantage of these puddles is that I don't have to give Seraphine water in her bowl. Her food and water bowls have screw-on lids that I am constantly opening and closing when she wants a feed or a drink: if they are left open, it's never long before ants and other insects invade in their hundreds.

The message for the week is always special, and Brigitte's words are something my thoughts are drawn back to in the days after I read it. Another adventure together in Oz – I hope so!

I shot a kangaroo about six days ago when it appeared close to camp in the first grey light of the day, and the meat has been delicious. I cooked the last of it yesterday and kept today's portion under my bedroll on the cruiser or in the shade in a plastic container. Storing it in these cooler places has meant that my meat has been keeping for up to a week, which is great.

There are plenty of roos in this country. Large mobs of them, occasionally hundreds strong, bound along in front of me with an ease and economy of effort that makes me feel slow and cumbersome. Despite their pace, they are not hard to shoot with my .303 rifle, though I may want to leave this gun behind at some stage as it is much heavier than my small .22 rifle. Anyway, north of the Dingo Fence the kangaroos are rare, as the young are very vulnerable and prey to packs of dingoes.

A few stumpies (lizards) may be in order tonight as there are heaps of them about; big ones too. In general the gathering has been monotonous: saltbush, ruby saltbush greens and fruit, mistletoe, samphire, pigweed. Nevertheless, it is an important part of my diet along with the meat I hunt and the 'carbos' I brought along.

I gather fruits and greens on the march, waiting until I see a particularly healthy and lush plant before gathering it for my pot.

This journey is all-consuming: there is little time for much else but the here and now of movement and survival. It is a pure feeling that goes back to our time as semi-nomadic hunter gatherers. I may have some modern equipment with me, but essentially this mission is a very simple journey of me travelling across the landscape finding water and food as I go.

DAY 23: THURSDAY, 7 JUNE
Depot Creek (Scott River), Lake Torrens

Another great day on the mission. As expected, I had a late get-away because I first needed to check the levels and quality of the puddles and creek pools. The puddles had almost all dried up but the pools in the creek were still fresh. I put my money on finding good water here at Depot Creek so I left this morning with just 5 litres. It paid off, but the very first hint of brackish-ness has me thinking I should fill up here. There are no more 'creeks' between here and the top of Torrens, and just one 'watercourse' – dry, of course. A strong headwind has picked up, and that and some heavy ground made it difficult going, even with just 4 litres on board. There was a cold wind blowing out of the north and for the first time on the trip I didn't sweat while hauling. Well, at least my shirt didn't become totally saturated. It was definitely a low water usage day.

I have certainly relaxed into the trip now and am taking each day as it comes. Of course I constantly need to know what's coming, particularly where water is concerned, so I study my maps regularly, but beyond these more practical matters, my concern really is what's in front of me at the time. The immediate problem or job at hand requires all my energy and focus, whether it's hauling the cruiser, gathering food, or repairing equipment. I am mostly too busy with the present to dwell much on the Arunta (Simpson Desert), for example. It is a few lifetimes away, or may as well be.

So now I have a good experience of Torrens, its moods and character. I was hoping to traverse it from east to west and back as a side trip to the mission, but that will have to wait. Even so, I have only Lake Mackay to visit to have experienced Australia's five largest lakes, all salt. They are each so unique. Mackay is the most remote by a long way, situated on the Western Australia – Northern Territory border. It was discovered by the Europeans in about 1930, by air, and has many islands. Its remoteness and terrain would make it a grand adventure.

Oh, I found another pen while ferreting through my gear. At this rate, I'll need it.

DAY 24: FRIDAY, 8 JUNE
Lake Torrens – neck of peninsula

Today I came around the big unnamed bay formed by the big unnamed peninsula. It was mostly difficult going with thick mats of low plants to haul over, small ravines to climb into and out of, and some sticky clay at the end of the bay – lovely. We passed an old car wreck on our march and I couldn't resist jumping in with Seraphine and pretending we were going for a little drive. It is going about as fast as we seem to be.

I am now camped on a saddle between dunes, from where I can see Torrens both east and west of me. To get here, I had a difficult climb; never easy at the end of the day. The good news is that hunting was successful today, so we are gorging on rabbit meat – yum. I usually cook rabbit in the big alloy pot, using it as a camp oven. It has a large lid that overhangs the sides, and I place the pot on a bed of hot coals as well as putting a few burning embers on the lid. It roasts my meal perfectly.

DAY 25: SATURDAY, 9 JUNE
Lake Torrens

I walked for 7 hours and covered 24 kilometres. That's a trip record. Occasionally the going was okay, but mostly the short slope between the lake and the foredune summit ridge was cut by many ravines, which I had to negotiate every 100 metres or so. It was extremely demanding and the last couple of hours really took it out of me. Still, I did enjoy the struggle and now I can just see the far shore of the lake to my north-west. That's definitely a sign that Torrens is coming to an end.

This stage of the Great Mission has been the third-most-difficult walk I've done, behind the Walk to Nowhere and the South Pole trek. I keep wondering, will the going be as demanding up ahead? More massive efforts for mediocre advances? I hope not; this is all so slow.

During this whole walk I haven't once been able to see a light from where I have been camped. I did see the glow of Port Augusta, or perhaps it was the Thomas Playford Power Station which supplies electricity for Adelaide, but that was during the first few days of the trip. Such isolation can be strangely haunting – not frightening, but friendly and thought-provoking.

I am fast running out of lake now and in a few more days I will leave it for the next stage, the Gibber Plains, a completely different landscape. Gibbers are rocks that have been rounded and polished by the elements over vast periods over time. In many places they completely cover the ground, so one walks on a carpet of rocks. Far from being difficult going with the cruiser, the gibber plain is mostly easy hauling as the rocks are usually small (about the size of nuts in their shells) and the cruiser rolls over them easily. Only occasionally are they larger (from the size of apples right up to boulders), which does make for harder going. The thought of new terrain has me quite excited: I was beginning to wonder whether the lake would just go on into infinity.

Seraphine dug a massive hole when we got here, really going for it in a rabbit warren right where we are camped. It was hilarious every time she came out all covered in sand. But I shouldn't have laughed, the warren is active and I camped here deliberately, with the hope that she would provide us with dinner. I closed all the escape routes of the warren by caving in their entrances. Then I set up camp and did my chores, checking on Seraphine's progress every now and then by pulling her out and reaching into the warren with my arm. After several hours, when I was beginning to think it was a lost cause, she became increasingly excited, yelping and digging with renewed vigour. I dragged her out and rewarded her efforts by pulling out not one, but two rabbits. My beautiful little companion bristled with pride and I showered her with love and affection and as much as she could eat!

DAY 26: SUNDAY, 10 JUNE
Lake Torrens

The question I am asking right now is, will it piss down again? It sure looks like it; the clouds have been building up all day. Rain isn't what I want at all, but I'll make the best of either situation.

Again today there were some good bits and some very difficult bits. I started along the shore and then on some good gravel just up from the shore. I hadn't come across this surface before and it made for very good going indeed, but not for long. Despite the difficulty of climbing down into, and then up out of, the numerous dry watercourses and gutters, or perhaps because of them – because of the challenge they offer – I am having an incredible time.

Yesterday evening I mentioned not seeing lights, but later in the night I noticed a glow. It came from the opal-mining town of Andamooka, and it is there again tonight, across on the western side of the lake and far away. It's amazing how much light we seem to need back in the 'unreal' world, and the lengths to which we will go to ensure its supply. Our towns and cities are lit up so much that they are visible from massive distances, glowing on the horizon. Energy is wasted by so many, with no thought about where it comes from and what the true cost of it is. I suspect that only in the future, with the benefit of hindsight, will people look back and realise how much of our resources we squandered. I don't have that luxury of supply out here, however. I only have one set of batteries for my head torch so I must conserve them. With the shortest day of the year approaching, I have no choice but to do some of my work by the light of the fire.

And now it's raining! For how long? How much? Will I have to wait for it to dry a bit? Maybe it will stop soon and go away. I must relax more about the weather.

DAY 27: MONDAY, 11 JUNE
Lake Torrens

We are held up again. It rained most of last night and although the rain wasn't heavy, it amounted to a lot of water and once again I am going nowhere. This is my 27th day out here and already I have spent eight days going nowhere (or just about) due to wet ground. As always I see the positives: I can have a rest and there is a well-watered route waiting for me ahead. I have carried too much water these past few days, as many small claypans contain good water, which should last a good few days yet. As for the gibber ahead, my experience is limited. If the plains have had these past two rains I expect the water-holes on the map to hold water, but are there other sources? I imagine so. Time will tell.

I saw two red kangaroos boxing this morning and filmed them for a bit. Red kangaroos are the largest of the species, and two adult males fighting is an impressive sight. They box with their arms, though the most powerful hits come when they sit back on their tails and kick with their legs. An evenly matched pair can fight for well over half an hour – and just like a fight in a ring, there is 'time out' every few minutes.

A few spots of rain have been falling throughout the day and heavy rain still looks threatening. I went for a wander to check on the ground surface and it is very heavy and spongy. Not great for the cruiser, but with all the water around I'll probably only need to carry 2 to 4 litres.

The day's rest has done my body good, and mentally it has helped feed the desire to see this traverse through.

DAY 28: TUESDAY, 12 JUNE
Lake Torrens

Rain started again about midnight, and is still falling at midday with no end in sight. I am relaxing in bed by reading, mind surfing and doing bits and pieces such as cleaning the cameras and repairing the stuff sacks. These things can be so absorbing that it is easy to lose yourself completely in them, and then be surprised by where you are when you finally emerge. My thoughts today are mostly questions: What big lessons will the Great Mission teach me? How will it change me? Will it become just another trip or will it stand out somehow from the others? How far will I go? Will all of me make it home or will a slice of me remain, cast adrift to wander permanently in isolation?

It has rained all day and I have been stuck 'indoors', under my brown tarpaulin. Outside it is grey, dark, wet, windy and cold but inside the atmosphere is nice and homely, and I am lying back and thinking homely thoughts. Is the fire going in the living area at home? Has Brigitte just made her afternoon coffee? Is she right now sitting in front of it, feet up on the table, munching on a biscuit? What of my parents? Are they well?

67

It can be a long time without news on expeditions such as this, and always at the back of my mind is the thought that I may return to some tragic news of friends and family. It is a dangerous world out there and nothing ever stays the same. In many respects I feel my own situation is safer. Here I have just the natural world to deal with, out there are people and people are the most dangerous animal on the planet. I always feel safest when not surrounded by them.

I'm carrying photos of all of my family: my twin sister and her children, my brother, my parents and grandparents. I'm also carrying a picture that shows my father's father on leave during World War I. He spent the whole war in the trenches on the Western Front. I often look at this picture, and in it I see a man of great strength and resilience of both mind and body. It always reminds me that things could be worse, that my life is a fortunate one, and that I should make the most of every moment.

When I am marching, I think more about action. I dream about future projects and adventures. When I am forced to stay still, I think more of home. That is not to say that while engaged in one, I don't dwell on and long for the other. I need both to strike a meaningful balance in my life and knowing that allows me maximum enjoyment from whatever I am currently engaged in.

It is now getting dark and the rain hasn't stopped for a moment. This is starting to feel like a mountaineering expedition: bad weather – halt; fine weather returns – wait a while for the snow to settle, or, in this case, the surface to dry a little.

Also, I did not get out of bed all day, today. Apart from general rest, the great benefit of doing this is that when I don't move I don't eat much, and I need to save my supplies. With a low food intake there is no need to go to the toilet. I pee in my bowl, just like when I am mountain climbing, and I toss the contents out in the rain. Should I be concerned about an avalanche, I wonder, if this weather continues?!

'For me this expedition is a mission that has to succeed.' This is Alain Hubert discussing his traverse of Antarctica. The quote is from *In the Teeth of the Wind*, which I am currently reading, and is a welcome contrast to a quote from another book I have with me: 'This mission cannot succeed.' Major General Stanislaw Sosabowski, commander of the Polish Parachute Brigade, said these words while talking about a plan to capture Arnhem Bridge from the Germans, in 1944. Arnhem Bridge, on the Rhine, links the Netherlands with Germany. The mission did not succeed!

DAY 29: WEDNESDAY, 13 JUNE
Lake Torrens

This is my third and hopefully last day at this camp. It is a nice though desolate spot situated in a small stand of acacias about 3 metres high. They are the only trees on a long, flat plain of saltbush, a low shrub 30 centimetres tall. Three hundred metres to the west is the lake and 1 kilometre east is a low sand ridge. The rain and low cloud-cover have given the place a barren, lonely appearance, though my heart is full of joy to be out here.

The rain stopped in the early hours of the morning, well mostly, and now the sun is out. Err, mostly. I have had a wash and spent a while reorganising everything, which must be done occasionally when things become a chaotic jumble. I also cleaned my guns, charged the camera batteries with the help of my solar panel and cleaned the lenses, cleaned my clothes, did some sewing and watched, as the day went by, the thin film of water that covers the lake start to disappear. An emu headed out there this morning, bound for the far shore. I often wonder why wildlife heads across these massive, barren salt lakes. Most of the time you can't see the far shore, and there is nothing in the middle, no food, no water.

The sun is doing wonders out there now but I know that tomorrow I will still be clearing mud as I move through heavy ground. In some places I'll be dodging puddles. Sometimes all the tiny claypans are full and I have to weave a lot to stay on bridges between them. Still, the sun today will have dried these bridges and I'll be carrying less than 3 litres of water. I'm running low on meat though, and need to go hunting again.

DAY 30: THURSDAY, 14 JUNE
Salt Creek, Lake Torrens

I've just realised I forgot to read Brigitte's message on Day 28.

'Victory awaits him who has everything in order' –
Amundsen

Day 30! And I have only had 20 days of full marching. Oh well, it hasn't been too much of a problem, on rainy days I have hardly touched my rations. Are things in order? They seem to be. Today I marched a record distance: 27 kilometres over the ground (20 kilometres as the crow flies), in 7.5 hours. If the ground had been dry, I think it would have taken 6.5 or 6 hours to cover the same distance. The terrain was the best I have experienced along the whole lake, with broad, fairly level terraces with little undulation, and quite open, low, salt-tolerant vegetation that is easy to weave around. The shore was okay to walk on, but again my cruiser invariably got bogged after a kilometre or three. Still, I really didn't expect to get here today, to the cusp of a new stage, the Gibber Plains. The next 10 to 15 kilometres up this salt creek is a bit of an intermission, I suppose. It's something completely different from either the rocks ahead or the flat brown of the lake behind. Lake Torrens took 19 days, with 300 kilometres walked and a lot of rain. This rain did allow me to complete the lake, however, by providing me with drinking water, for which I am thankful.

It was another successful hunt today, so we have fresh meat again. I caught a roo, which will feed us for a week. Meat is the richest and most easily abundant bush food here, so we are eating heaps of it. Never before in my life have I eaten so much meat. I dice and mix a huge amount with the evening meal of rice and local greens. Then I cook a large number of steaks, to be eaten whenever, over the next 24 hours. How about one at the break of day? Yes! How about one just before sleep time? Sure! I just can't stop, so I don't. With all this mention of steaks, I've just had another!

I am camped about a kilometre from the wide entrance to this beautiful salty creek and from here I can see the lake. Watching Torrens go from being completely covered yesterday morning to almost completely dry this evening has been pure magic. Strips of wet and dry one behind the other, constantly changing as I move along and the surface dries off. For three weeks the lake has been my constant companion. I've loved it and cursed it, but mostly simply enjoyed it. Tomorrow I'll leave it behind and head north into a very different landscape, a world of stone.

Thirty days have just flown by. Will I speed up? I have to. On studying my map just now, I don't think I'll be on the gibber plains till the day after tomorrow as the next 25 kilometres could be difficult.

My plan for the gibber plains is simple: I must stay low and link a series of waterholes that lie on my route. So I won't be heading directly to Muloorina Station, but will be doing a big arc that means I don't have to climb up and down the hills, mountains and plateaus that occur to my north. I have to say, I am excited by the thought of heading off across the shimmering stones towards a mirage that looks like never ending.

SIMPSON DESERT

Burt Waterhole

Tepaminkanie
Waterhole

Goyder
Lagoon

BIRDSVILLE
INSIDE
TRACK

Ck

Sturt
Stony
Desert

Macumba

R

Warburton

TRACK

Wadlarkaninna
Waterhole

Kalamurra
Lake

Neales R

Lake
Eyre
North

Lake Jeanine

Cooper

Lake
Puntawolona

Ck

BIRDSVILLE

Tirari
Desert

Clayton

N

OODNADATTA

TRACK

Lake Eyre
South

Frome

Muloorina

Dingo

R

Fence

R

0   50km

Hermit Hill

Mount
Alford

Marree

Map 2

Davenport
Ck

+Cadnia Hill

Willouran Ra

+
Mount
Norwest

Salt Ck

Lake
Torrens

+
Termination
Hill

Andamooka

Jon's route ――――

MAP 2: LAKE TORRENS TO EYRE CREEK

3

LAKE TORRENS TO LAKE EYRE

Into a World of Stone

DAY 31: FRIDAY, 15 JUNE
Flagstaff Waterhole? Flagstaff Lake!

June 15 is my summit day for a series of Indian Himalaya peaks: Kedarnath Dome, in 1985; Shivling, in 1986; and a lot of the traverse of the Kedarnath Peaks, in 1987. Indeed, it's a lucky day for me and never passes without my mind wandering back to the great days of my youth, climbing alone under a full moon to that special place where the earth and heaven meet.

What a struggle I had today coming up Salt Creek. I got bogged many times, and when I wasn't stopped it was constantly heavy going. It nearly destroyed me; for a while anyway. I am now camped by Flagstaff Waterhole, which has swollen to the size of a lake, 500 to 600 metres wide and 2 to 3 kilometres long. I have the best site on the whole shore, by some pretty dunes about 15 metres from the water's edge.

This place feels like the edge of a new world, so completely different from the last that it may as well be another planet. To the north-east is the Willouran Range and to the north, where I'm headed, are a number of flat-topped little conical mountains. Between them and me, there is a vast plain that I think is quite vegetated. I'm navigating more with the compass now that I am no longer simply following the Lake. I've taken a bearing for tomorrow and one of the little mountains is directly in my line of travel. Hopefully I'll reach it tomorrow night. On the way I should pass an unnamed waterhole. Despite conditions being difficult, Salt Creek was beautiful, particularly down near its terminus, at Lake Torrens. There were some striking boulders in the middle of salty pools, and beautiful dunes scattered about.

DAY 32: SATURDAY, 16 JUNE
plateau ridge line

What a camp site! I am up on a ridge top, a flat-topped, level crest, 10 to 20 metres wide and 6 kilometres long, which extends south from one of the plateaus that abound here. The ridge looked like it would give level, dry conditions, and it does, mostly. Even up here there are small pools holding up to 5 litres. Fortunately there is always a way around them. The great thing about this route is the view from up here. I find the vistas from places like this equal to any I have been fortunate enough to witness. I just *love* these rounded conical hills. They seem otherwldly, and to me they speak of great age. In this respect I am reduced to a momentary shadow, which feels good. Finally, the Flinders Ranges seem to have disappeared, as has Mount Deception. I can still see Termination Hill, though, and to my east are Mount Norwest and the Willouran Range.

Today was another very hard day for a reward of just 14 kilometres as the crow flies. Will I ever speed up? Maybe only when I start leaving behind caches of equipment. This will be some time from now but I look forward to it greatly. Meanwhile, I plod slowly north. I am seriously hampered by rain, heavy wet ground, and bogs. Repeatedly getting bogged is a horrid nightmare. It challenges you physically, to get out of the bog, but it also challenges your will, your drive, your determination, and perhaps even your sanity. Often you don't even see the danger coming, then suddenly you are on it – a surface of just the wrong consistency that clogs the wheels immediately. Other times it happens more slowly, building up and up until the wheels finally jam. When they stop turning, one must either drag the cruiser out, if it's only a few more steps, then clean off the mud *or* stop and clean repeatedly until you are clear of boggy ground. The effort required to move a bogged cruiser is enormous, and seriously saps my strength. Sometimes I've had to clean the wheels six or seven times in the space of a few hundred metres. This is cramping my style more than anything else to date. The only compensation is . . . I don't have to carry water!

The other challenge to my time and energy levels today was crossing the Vermin-Proof Fence. The fence stands about 1.5 metres high with its base buried in the ground. Going over it involved a complete unload. Well that took some time, and I know the Dingo Fence is just north of here and I'll have to do it all again!

DAY 33: SUNDAY, 17 JUNE
Clark Creek

Hey, a good day, I only got bogged twice! I crossed the Dingo Fence too, where the ridge reached the main plateau. This fence is also about 1.5 metres high and was difficult with the cruiser. At about 6000 kilometres long, the Dingo Fence is the world's longest fence. It runs from the head of the Great Australian Bight to Jandowae in central Queensland and keeps the dingoes out of the sheep country to the south. It is constantly maintained: every section is driven along once a fortnight and different people are responsible for different sections.

The going has been good, over compact solid gibber, and the scenery has been superb, with mesas and conical hills. All around is a feast of vivid colours, mostly red and green but also yellow, white and purple. There are a lot of minerals here, shimmering in some places like gems.

Today the route was a bit better, for a change, perhaps because it was a bit drier. Despite this, one of the major creek lines I crossed was actually flowing. Fortunately there was a gibber and gravel ford near where I hit it and I was able to cross relatively easily.

Hermit Hill put in its first appearance today, and will be in sight for the next few days. Last night I saw Cadnia Hill and it is now looming larger. These hills are nothing like the size and height of the mountains I passed in the first weeks. However, they are features that remain in sight over a number of days and I get to enjoy them in their many moods. They have their own identity, personality I'd even say, although this will sound ridiculous to some. We share the landscape and it is always a little sad to say farewell when inevitably they slip from view. For most of the rest of this walk I won't have such companions, as there are no mountains or hills for a long stretch. I'm not worried – I'll find something else to befriend along the way.

DAY 34: MONDAY, 18 JUNE
just south of the Oodnadatta Track

Another good run. Will it become a habit? I hope so. I encountered all sorts of terrain today, including creeks, lots of low ridges to walk over, two bogs, and then one creek which took me an hour. I had to unload on two difficult crossings. Fortunately the gibber was easier, though there were a few heavy areas.

I have been busy reorganising the load. Because of the abundance of water I have moved the empty 20-litre container to the underside of the tail shafts. I have also shifted stuff from the two front corners in front of the wheels to the middle of the cruiser. I think this will be better in bogs, too, as the mud won't have anything to pile against. Another bonus is that now nothing obstructs me from reaching the wheels with my ski pole, so I can clean mud off without getting out of the harness.

I am camped now in a beautiful creek bed (dry of course!) that is lined with gums. Mostly gravel, the bigger creeks are the easiest for me to cross and I am hoping Davenport Creek, on the north side of the Oodnadatta Track, will be as straightforward as this one.

DAY 35: TUESDAY, 19 JUNE
Morris Creek

Davenport Creek was a nightmare to cross! I had to ferry everything in batches over about 50 metres of swampy marsh and the whole exercise took 2.5 hours. Afterwards I ran down between Davenport and Alberrie creeks to Charles Angus Bore, then went on a bearing for Muloorina Station over the gibber ridge to a lovely little waterhole, here at Morris Creek. The terrain was mostly very good, but again I lost much time in getting bogged. The new load arrangement works well and several times today I was able to clear the wheels by just leaning over and scrapping them with my ski pole while staying harnessed in. A bit of reversing often helped.

Crossing the creeks that flowed into the salt lake was always a trial.
Depot Creek, Lake Torrens, 7 June.

In stony country south of the Tirari Desert, 24 June. These flat areas provided the fastest
travel of the journey.

Desalinating water on the Cooper Creek, 27 June.

Catching up on domestics during a rest day at Wadlarkaninna Waterhole, Warburton Creek, 1 July.

When rain or heavy dew threatened I slept under my tarp, which was set up to collect the precious water.

I saw evidence of past Aboriginal occupation of the land every day of the walk. Here I am examining a grindstone and its grinder. Warburton Creek, 12 July.

Many times during the first seventy days, the cruiser became bogged while crossing otherwise 'dry' watercourses.

Salty pools of water, such as this one, provided relief for the eyes in a world of sandridges.

A chance meeting with Aboriginal stockmen who were on a cattle muster, 3 August.

Bloated bovine! Despite the fact that this cow had been dead awhile and was bloated and partly crawling with maggots, the meat was tasty and welcome.

Picking sandalwood berries (fruit) on the banks of the Georgina River.

I baked a small damper once or twice a week, usually adding some native fruit to the dough.

I gathered vegetables, fruits and nuts to supplement the carbos I carried and the meat I hunted.

Seraphine on the dry bed of the Mulligan River, 8 August.

The strain of the previous eighty-five days showing on my face.
Mulligan River, 8 August.

After spending ninety days in arid desert country, this was the first time I had seen massive trees. Georgina River, 19 August.

Me on the dry rock bed of the Georgina River, after swapping the cruiser for the 'Beast' (my pack), 25 August.

Contemplating the tidal salt water of Albert River and journey's end. Burketown, 20 September.

The local schoolkids presented me with a banner they had made, and walked the final 500 metres of the march with me.

Brigitte made this headstone, which we placed on Seraphine's grave during the long drive home.

I'm about 42 to 43 kilometres from Muloorina Station so I would have to put in my best days so far to get there in two days. I don't think I'll bother setting it as a goal, but if the terrain is good and I don't get bogged it will happen naturally. There is less chance of bogging for two reasons: the ground is drying out every day, and there are fewer creeks to cross on this last stretch of gibber. So maybe two days is possible, but I won't overdo anything just to get there sooner.

Wow, Day 35, a message from Brigitte!

'I am with you, every step of the way, my love. Always.'

You bet!

When I get to the station it will be strange to be in the world of people again, even briefly. After weeks or months alone, I enter a different sort of reality. I feel sometimes that I am the only person on the planet, and the idea of communicating with others can be daunting. Will we be able to communicate verbally, or have I forgotten how? Of course deep down I know I haven't, but after many weeks alone strange thoughts and ideas do begin to circulate and some of them can take root, even in the most rational part of my mind. I do look forward to speaking with Brigitte though.

I have promised myself a holiday camping down on the Frome River, at Muloorina. It will be good to catch up with Colleen and Malcolm Mitchell as well. I first met them in 1996 when I came this way for my Walk to Nowhere and have

81

visited several times since. Malcolm has lived here all his life; he knows the place like the back of his hand and has a particular affinity with Lake Eyre. Malcolm remembers well the time when, as a child, he met Donald Campbell, who established a land-speed record on the dry lake bed in 1964. Malcolm and Colleen are a wealth of information and wonderful people as well.

Things to do! A serious sort is on the list. I'll be leaving a few things here, and I need to go through everything carefully. I'll have to make calls from the station, to Brigitte, Mum and Dad; write letters; and have a clean. It would also be nice to find time for a lie in, even just till sunrise one day!

Ah, I can see the zodiac light. Or is it the celestial light? The latter is dust in the solar system that gets picked up by the sun's rays. It is clearly visible as a broad column of light from the horizon where the sun has set or will rise to the zenith. It lasts several hours. Some nights the light is just so clear and powerful. I have seen it elsewhere in Australia, but it's never as bright as here, in the outback. The lights reassure me, they welcome me, they make me feel at home.

DAY 36: WEDNESDAY, 20 JUNE
near 2 mile tank, 23 km from Muloorina Station

Another desperate day on the mission. I would be doing at least 2 or 3 kilometres a day more if it wasn't for this mud. In places you sink straight to your ankles. Again today, I wasted a lot of time and a massive amount of energy on one river crossing. This quagmire was 50 metres across with several flowing channels. The whole thing had obviously been completely swamped during the rains. I had to unload the back half of the cruiser and ferry things across, which is exhausting work in this heavy, sticky mud. Then I re-crossed the Dingo Fence and tomorrow morning I'll have to do it again, but this time I'll go through a gate on a nearby track. Because the fence squiggles all over the place and so do I, I'll end up going through it three times.

Marching on the gibber itself was mostly very good. Of course, I had to collect a few nice rock samples.

My friends of the past few days have slipped from view as I lose more altitude and the intervening ridges hide the small mountains. I did still get some glimpses of the Willouran Range though.

An addition to my list of things to do at Muloorina: check over the cruiser and tighten all the bolts. I noticed that the shaft brace has come undone on one side. Hmm, it looks like the screws there just sheared off. Muloorina will definitely be a working holiday!

DAY 37: THURSDAY, 21 JUNE
Frome River, Muloorina

Yippee! I have just done my biggest day yet in both time and distance as the crow flies, and made it to Muloorina. I dropped in to see Colleen, my first person since Brigitte left 36 days ago! Colleen gave me a hug and a kiss and some mail. I have a letter from each of Brigitte, Mum, Greg and Eric. It is a beautiful letter from my love with a few pictures of the unclimbed mountains in Antarctica that she hopes to visit. I called Brigitte from the Mitchell's phone but she was not there so I left a message on the answering machine and will try again tomorrow.

The run to get here was a straighter route without too much weaving. It was also my first 8-hour march since I left Port Augusta, though until the days get longer, I think I'll keep it mostly to 7.5. Also, I didn't film today which always takes a slice (15 minutes minimum) from my day. I saw two emus as I crossed a flat pebbly swale near here. They snuck up on Seraphine and me, and I only noticed them when they were 10 metres away. They followed us along till we climbed up and over the dune, the male leading and the hen following 5 metres behind. It was beautiful. I collected a few more gibbers as I had limited myself to only two particularly interesting ones yesterday. Today I picked up a 'marble collection' of lovely little round ones.

Overall it was a nice day's walk with lots of variety of landscape, from gibber, to dunes, to savannah, to the Frome River, which still has a strong flow. It is just wonderful to be camped here, in deep shade by clear flowing water. This is the most luxuriant place I've seen on the walk so far: it's a perfect place for the mind and body to rest after the rigour of the past five weeks.

Colleen informs me that Muloorina has had 75 millimetres of rain over the past few weeks. To the west there has been even more and both the Macumba and Neals rivers are flowing into Lake Eyre. No one lives in the Tirari Desert, north of here, so there are no figures, but the rains were so widespread consensus is some must have fallen there. I'll get a clearer picture of things when I have a yarn to Malcolm, who is out somewhere on this vast cattle station.

The big questions on my mind now are: How long will the Tirari Desert claypans hold water? And will the Clayton River crossing take all day? After all this rain, claypans in the desert will now be mostly full and if they hold water for 10 days or so I will be able to traverse this normally waterless desert carrying no water at all. This will save me hauling the weight of 40 litres of water, and mean using less energy and taking less time to cross the desert. I imagine there will be difficult decisions to make along the way as day-by-day the pools of shallow water shrink due to evaporation and soakage. Also because of the rains, the usually dry Clayton River will have big pools of water divided by large areas of soft mud. It's very wide and I have serious concerns that crossing it may take all day – if I need to ferry everything across, it certainly will.

DAY 38: FRIDAY, 22 JUNE
Frome River, Muloorina

I've had a great day. I spoke to Brigitte on the phone, as well as getting a fax from her. I did some work on my equipment, wrote four letters and washed most of my clothes. Then I had a few great yarns with Colleen and Malcolm about the route ahead and water, of course, plus fishing and making sausages! Malcolm and the team were getting ready for his youngest daughter Leanne's 21st birthday, and were in the process of making hundreds of sausages. The party will be held in the giant shearing shed and, as is common in this big country, many of the guests will fly here in their own planes, from hundreds of kilometres away.

My concerns of a few days ago, regarding seeing and communicating with people again, seem slightly over the top. I feel confident and relaxed in the company of this family, though intensely aware of every word and gesture. Regardless of this, I do feel that I've built a shell around myself over these past weeks and that too much human interaction could well crack it open. The only assistance I receive is to use the phone, to let my family know of my whereabouts and safety.

It's a beautiful place, this camp site by the river, and it is simply magic to be out on a trip like this, slowly moving across the continent. I'm happy and content – there is nowhere I'd rather be and nothing I'd rather be doing.

DAY 39: SATURDAY, 23 JUNE
Frome River, Muloorina

My holiday is at an end and I've done everything I wanted to. It has been just beautiful to work and rest peacefully down here with nobody about. I'm leaving behind my .303 rifle and the rocks I collected in the few days before I arrived here. The .303 was a hard call and it means I won't be able to hunt large game, such as feral camels, donkeys and large pigs, but I'm desperate to lighten my load and will just have to make do with my smaller single shot .22 rifle. I'm also leaving my maps covering the country south of here and Alain Hubert's book of Antarctica.

I tried some fishing earlier today but had no luck. I've brought some light fishing line, which is wrapped around Seraphine's eating bowl, and some hooks and sinkers. Fish will be a welcome addition to my diet and I am hoping the Warburton Creek will be better. I've gorged myself on the bulrush since I arrived though, and am taking some along for the next few days. It is a fantastic water green and I am glad I can stock up on it.

It is going to be a shock to the senses to go from this peaceful oasis that is full of life to Lake Eyre tomorrow and the Tirari Desert the day after. I will be changing planets again.

DAY 40: SUNDAY, 24 JUNE
Lake Eyre

I am camped about 500 metres east of the shore of Lake Eyre and interestingly, I am below sea level. Being here brings back memories from last year's trip, as Brigitte and I camped in an almost identical location just a few kilometres east. Tomorrow, God willing, I'll hit the Tirari. The Tirari Desert lies between Lake Eyre to the west and the Strzelecki and Sturt Stony deserts to the east, and between the Clayton River to the south and the Warburton Creek to the north. It is a parallel sand ridge desert, 200 kilometres long and 100 kilometres wide. The dune system begins properly about 10 kilometres from the Clayton River, the crossing of which might take a hell of a long time.

Today was wonderful. I climbed up and out of the Frome River and travelled for 15 kilometres on a beautiful surface: small pebbles over level, hard sand. It was perfect and I hit 4.5 kilometres per hour, but things changed as I dropped down to Lake Eyre. The going was slow and laborious, as I knew it would be, but I could appreciate the beauty of this area at the same time.

I spent 40 minutes filming today, as I wanted a few more shots of me walking over the stony country, and will do some more tomorrow. I've got to accept it and get it done but sometimes it is such a chore. With a subject (someone else) it's much, much easier but most of the shots I take out here require the use of the tripod, which needs to be set up and then the camera attached to it. Then I must clip on the microphone, using the 10 metre extension lead, and place this close to the action but out of the frame. If it's a long shot of me on the march I must harness up, switch on the camera and then march across the frame (or away from it or towards it). For close shots of me doing things such as writing, repairing, skinning a rabbit or any one of the hundred and one things I do every day, I usually shoot the action from several angles; over the shoulder, a wide shot and an extreme close-up. All of this plus the careful packing away of the camera means it takes a long time to get just 30 seconds of film, and I'm hoping to shoot 25 hours! However, despite the extra workload, and my occasional grumbling, I am actually very motivated to film this mission.

It is a joy to be on the move again, though the two days off were just perfect. My body feels well rested and strong, and if I continue to find water, I should be able to cross this little desert quickly. On the other hand, there is no point in overdoing things. Lots of little milestones today: Stage Three over, 40 days out, and I just clicked over 600 kilometres.

4

THE TIRARI DESERT

Playing Dare

DAY 41: MONDAY, 25 JUNE
Tirari Desert

So once again, here I am. It was less than a year ago that Brigitte and I were here and it feels fantastic to return. This will be my third unsupported traverse of the desert and Seraphine's second. The only other person who's done it in the past 100 years is Brigitte. Anyway, I'm really very happy to be back. The terrain will be mostly swales, or inter-dunal corridors, with low shrubs and some stands of various acacias and gums up to 3-metres high. It is usually slightly undulating, with claypans in the low-lying areas and salt lakes scattered throughout the desert. Overall the going should be fast, in fairly straight lines.

The crossing of the Clayton took 2.5 hours and went smoothly. I unloaded a whole heap of stuff on the south bank and ferried things across the water. This is the deepest water the cruiser has been in, and it came up to the top of the wheels.

On the bottom of the river, I was sinking up to my ankles in mud at times, but luckily the lightened cruiser floated just above the surface of the mud! From the river, the 8 or so kilometres to the beginning of the dune field were slow ones, just like last year. Small, solid tussocks everywhere made for very bumpy, slow, uneven going. Fortunately, once I hit the dunes my speed instantly improved. And there is water! I see pools every 3 or 4 kilometres, mostly in the obvious places but, as usual, sometimes in unlikely places with small or almost non-existent catchments. Strange.

I really ripped along this afternoon and felt very strong indeed, so now I'm wondering just how long this traverse of the Tirari will take. I'd like to go for it as this ground water won't hold for long. Once on the Warburton Creek, water shouldn't be an issue, though according to Malcolm it won't flow for much longer and once it stops, the water in the main channel will soon turn to salt.

Up to this point, the trip has required so much energy of both mind and body that there has been little time for thoughts of the outside world. I have enjoyed that, but could it be that having been thrown in the deep end at the start, with difficult terrain and boggy conditions, things will now begin to flow a bit more easily? I think so. Not that from here on will be a dream run, but ironically what slowed me down before, the rain and mud along with the terrain, now means I've got the best of both worlds – a dry run, mostly, with water in claypans.

When I entered the dune system earlier today, it was at

exactly the same point as Brigitte and I did last year. Was that by chance? I'm not sure. I guess my navigation is pretty spot-on at the moment, but I wasn't trying to be especially accurate as any one of four or five swales would have done me. I recognised this one immediately. We had a break here and I climbed a dune.

These days I am getting a long, solid night's sleep and in the mornings I always feel ready for what the day might bring.

DAY 42: TUESDAY, 26 JUNE
Tirari Desert

Message day today, so here goes . . .

'What drives men over polar regions is the power of the
unknown over the human spirit.' Nansen

I won't be sure how much of the Tirari I've covered until I hit 'Lake Seraphine', but today was my biggest day yet, certainly as the crow flies. I enjoyed it immensely. It is amazing how familiar some sections of this walk are, and they are almost always the good, open, fast sections. But there is also the unknown – this trip is full of it. I suppose life is like that too, all a big unknown, yet we constantly attempt to remove that unknown from our daily life using routine.

Up until now the ponds on this route have all been small

with a maximum diameter of 8 metres, but here in the Tirari there is lots of water. In the big open swale where I am camped is a 100-metre long pond and from a dune top earlier, I saw four or five more ponds, not as big as this one but still much bigger than anything south. This is good news, and although it in no way guarantees more water ahead, it is a very positive indicator.

This journey just keeps blowing me away, in the beauty that surrounds me with every step, the little surprises around every corner and the changing light as the sun moves slowly from horizon to horizon. A large part of me had expected to fail in my Mission before getting this far, yet I'm still here, I'm still going strong and things are looking good. A rising sense of optimism is creeping into my soul.

DAY 43: WEDNESDAY, 27 JUNE
Cuttupirra Waterhole, Cooper Creek, Tirari Desert

It turns out I marched 24.5 kilometres as the crow flies yesterday, but the going was a bit more difficult today and I struggled a lot. I crossed Lake Seraphine, named by Brigitte and me last year. Well, officially it has no name but we felt like filling in a few blanks on our map.

Once I hit the Cooper I took a long route around the dry bed of the creek to reach this waterhole. It is beautiful here, at my camp at the base of the 'Big Dune'. Every 10 or 20 kilometres along the Cooper Creek, there is a dune which dwarfs all others around it, giving great views from its top. I remember this one from two previous visits. In fact, it was during my first visit, towards the end of the Walk to Nowhere, in 1996, that I decided it was time to attempt the Great Mission. Now finally, on my fourth attempt, I've made it this far. I hit 500 kilometres as the crow flies today – that's a quarter of the way!

I saw a lame camel as we descended to the creek. It probably slipped on soft mud. One of its front legs was near useless and it could hardly walk. Its struggle for life was almost over, and I was afraid it faced a slow, lingering death. I don't have my big gun anymore, so I couldn't put it out of its misery, and secure a new supply of dried meat at the same time. It was a hard call to leave the .303 at Muloorina, and one I regret now.

I did shoot a rabbit today, the first in a while. It was a wonderful change from my standard fare but for a big, hungry boy and a little, hungry dog the meat on a rabbit doesn't go far.

I have also been finding native pear since entering the desert, just as I did in 1996. This is a delicious green vegetable that is definitely one of my favourites. It is just as good as anything you might grow organically in your garden, and far superior to something you might buy in a supermarket. It grows on dune crests and should become a staple in my diet over the next 1000 kilometres or so. It also keeps very well.

The days have been perfect of late, crystal clear with not a cloud in the sky. Today a lovely wind from the east cooled me but I wasn't so keen on it when I hit the creek and headed straight into it.

My camp tonight is right near where all the cockatoos sleep on this creek; what a wonderful racket.

DAY 44: THURSDAY, 28 JUNE
Lake Puntawolona, Tirari Desert

Today I saw our tracks from last year in a few places. They had quite a powerful impression on me. To think I shall be seeing Brigitte shortly fills me with incredible excitement. There is a bit of trepidation too. Who will come with her and how will I cope? After they leave, will it be too difficult to get back to where I mentally am now? No, it should be fine. I'm relaxed about it and I don't think the visit will alter my focus.

Knowing the route and making some minor variations to last year's walk, I moved quickly around the bends of the Cooper. Along the way I saw a dingo. I hear their howls every night. It is a beautiful sound and I love it, but I do, of course, have serious concerns for Seraphine. I try to keep her as safe as possible but it is impossible to eliminate the risk entirely without tying her up constantly. This I won't do, of course, so we run the risk.

I went along a different and much better swale to get here from the Cooper than last year, with only one dune to cross. This swale took me to the best point on Lake Puntawolona and avoided the southern end, which is softer. The lake is in about the same condition as last year, a bit heavy but not too slow. I am hoping that last year's trend will continue as the next lake,

Lake Jeanine (also named by Brigitte and me), was better than this and Kalamurra the best of the lot.

I need to find water tomorrow morning and I am reasonably confident that the big clay slope at the northern end of Puntawolona should yield some. If not, I may have to climb a few dunes to have a look around and hopefully spot some.

I moved very well today and marched the record distance so far, but as the crow flies, I only went 14 kilometres! I headed south several times and also came a long way east as I negotiated the Cooper, which accounts for the discrepancy.

I found our tracks from last year in the clay area below the cliffs under Cuttupirra Dune. There was a tread pattern in a few spots, then later, on the surface of Puntawolona, footprints and wheel lines. Amazing. I guess they will have disappeared in another year's time, given that they are all but gone now.

There is a big pool of water on the lake and many different birds are calling and singing out there. I have swapped the heavy metal of the cockatoos last night for an orchestra tonight!

DAY 45: FRIDAY, 29 JUNE
Lake Jeanine, Tirari Desert

Another big day and again I saw our faint tracks many times. Tonight I am camped exactly where we did last year; a few charred sticks and a small pile of twigs are the only evidence of our stay here. It is a strange feeling, knowing that a year ago there was laughter and talk here, around the fire, then nothing but silence and the wind since. Until today.

The going was mostly good and the route relatively direct. The weather has been fabulous today, from the beautiful sunrise over one lake to the sunset here at Lake Jeanine. There is no fresh meat for tea tonight. Still, my dried meat is excellent and because up until now the hunting has been good I have a bit left. If I manage to get some large game or loads of fish I'd like to dry some more.

The water is drying up and I see less of it each day. The puddles are becoming fewer and smaller and although I'm sure larger ones still exist, they could be anywhere in this massive landscape. In terms of my water needs, I have been playing a game of dare. How far do I dare to go before I fill up my container? Of course, I do have the distiller and there are large pools in the centre of most of the salt lakes, but this is not an appealing option. Just to get to them means crossing hundreds of metres, sometimes several kilometres, of ankle-deep, salty sludge. And, of course, the water must then be distilled.

I think I have two days to go before I reach Warburton Creek and am looking forward to a few days off by a waterhole. I am also starting to cast my mind forward to the next stage, the march along the Warburton. As usual, I ask myself a million questions about it that only a combination of experience with the landscape and its current condition can answer. I'll have to be patient.

DAY 46: SATURDAY, 30 JUNE
Lake Kalamurra, Tirari Desert

I am not sure the day is over yet, perhaps I'll walk a bit more later. I have stopped an hour earlier than usual as it was getting very hot and I am short of water. I did manage to collect 6 litres today, so am fine for now but I will march tonight for a few hours to ensure I get to the river tomorrow. As I am now on Lake Kalamurra I should have a good run. We camped at this very spot last year and although the lake is much softer and heavier this year, a major flow poured into it right here just a few weeks ago so I'm hoping that once I have left this area things will improve. There is a half moon as well that will help.

Earlier on, a dingo came our way as we were having a break in a fairly open swale. The first I knew of it was when Seraphine leapt to action and ran straight for it barking loudly! It was 40 to 50 metres away and for a moment it just watched, then it fled at top speed for the closest dune. I yelled for Seraphine to stop, which she did about 100 metres away. She came back looking a bit confused, as if wondering why she might be in trouble when really she should have been given a medal.

I got water today from only three spots. Three tiny clay-pans had minuscule pools in camel pad depressions. There were only about 200 to 300 millilitres in each pad print and funny things swam in the brown ooze, but I sucked it all up into my mouth and then spat it into my water bottles. That water was the thickest drink I've ever had, but definitely the most satisfying, and my rice tonight is chocolatey and full of protein!

After a break, I went like a rocket for an hour and a half at sunset and into the night. I pushed hard and now I have no qualms about water: I will reach the security of the Warburton tomorrow. Going for it was the best plan.

DAY 47: SUNDAY, 1 JULY
Wadlarkaninna Waterhole, Warburton Creek

Yippee! I had an early start followed by a great day and ending with a beautiful evening. It is magic to be camped by water again, that giver of life.

The haul down Lake Kalamurra was just as I remembered it. I did the best bit last night, finishing it off this morning. From the lake, I took a different line than last year's, towards the creek. Once there, I enjoyed a long moment of immense satisfaction as I looked out over the Warburton floodplain. I had rocketed across the Tirari in great style, drawing heavily on my experience to employ tactics I wouldn't have had the confidence to contemplate in years gone by.

Once I hit the floodplain I got a roo, but what I'd really like is a nice fat duck. I'll try for one tomorrow. Within minutes of shooting the roo, birds of prey and crows appeared and by the time I left, 50 to 100 of them were circling and landing in a tree. Finally, just as I was going, a dingo/border collie cross turned up.

After the floodplain I stayed close to the end of the dunes and crossed some lovely claypans. They are mostly full and generally there is water everywhere. (More than last year when Brigitte and I were here.) There is much more exposed clay here than in the desert, which is why the claypans are full. Overall, the going on the floodplain is a bit slower than the Tirari.

I am now on the south side of Wadlarkaninna Waterhole at a beautiful camp site. I did a lap around the waterhole to find somewhere I was happy with, given it will be home for a few days. It is good to stop.

One third of the journey is now behind me and Stage Four is at an end. Also, I now have a holiday for maybe four days. Under normal circumstances I would only take one day, but I am two days early for my meeting with Brigitte. This forced stop is of little concern, except that I can't eat many carbos when I don't move as I simply don't carry any spare for idle days. Days without carbohydrates are very difficult and I notice on the days when I eat only meat, greens and fruit a general lethargy, with everything taking a far greater effort of will. Despite this feeling, I must still go out and hunt and gather food, collect water, cook, repair equipment, wash, film, etc.

5

THE WARBURTON CREEK

Desperate Days and
Rising Doubts

DAY 48: MONDAY, 2 JULY
Wadlarkaninna Waterhole, Warburton Creek

From my camp on the waterhole I walked over to the creek and
was surprised to see it still flowing – just, but flowing nonetheless. This changes my thinking slightly on the next few days
and I am not sure what to do. Should I stay here at this waterhole that is now isolated from the creek, or go and camp by the
main channel? Where will the best hunting and gathering be?
The best fishing will be here at the waterhole, so that's probably where I'll base myself.

We have two small ducks and one small fish for dinner
tonight. I can't complain about that. It's the first fish I've
caught on the mission and it's so nice to have a change. I put
my line in and caught it almost immediately, using a piece of
kangaroo meat as bait.

DAY 49: TUESDAY, 3 JULY
Stony Crossing, Warburton Creek

Well, my gear stayed at Wadlarkaninna but I have just walked the 17 kilometres to where I am due to meet Brigitte. From last year's walk I know there are no good camp sites up around here so I decided to come up with just my pack, sleeping bag and mat, and a little food, and I must say it was nice to walk without the cruiser for a change. I'll leave a note at the Stony Crossing road sign with directions to my temporary camp here. We prearranged this when I called Brigitte from Muloorina. But how long do I wait? Will she really come? As the sun went down tonight my doubts increased, but then I remembered her words, 'I'll be there, the third, at night.' I should try to relax. She will be here when she arrives, and if for some reason she hasn't been able to make it, so be it. I will know what to do, when to go.

I think back over my Tirari crossing. I took a slightly different route this year but at times walked over ground that Brigitte and I shared last year. Waiting now, at our last camp site from that trip, I am desperately trying to stay on an even keel about this meeting. I don't yet know whether I'm succeeding!

Tomorrow is Day 50 – 50 days to come one third of the distance to Burketown, including 15 days stuck waiting and 35 days of marching. Can I do the next third in 35? Yes. The last in 25? That would make 95 days of walking, but how many more days off will be imposed on me by this big country, I wonder.

102

DAYS 50-52: WEDNESDAY, 4 TO FRIDAY, 6 JULY
Wadlarkaninna Waterhole, Warburton Creek

She made it! Brigitte, an old mate of ours Phil Wilkins, and our new friend Tarne Malor arrived at Stony Crossing on the night of the 3rd, not long after dark. I heard a vehicle approach and stop up at the turnoff, 150 metres from where I was camped, followed by a whoop of joy – they had found my note buried under the signpost. Shortly after I was blinded by headlights as they approached and then surrounded by people as they piled out of the vehicle. I felt a little shell-shocked but we talked long into the night. Then, after just several hours sleep, I awoke at 2 a.m. and under an almost full moon, walked back alone to Wadlarkaninna Waterhole, leaving Brigitte with a map to my camp site. They drove down later, at a more civilized hour.

Now we are having a wonderful holiday by the waterhole. Brigitte asked Phil and Tarne along to witness the fact that she was not assisting me in any way. They have a pile of food and alcohol in the back of the car and help themselves discreetly to it. As for me, I have been getting ducks! They really are rich and for the first time on the trip I am not suffering from pangs of hunger. This is despite the fact that as always when not on the move, I eat no sugar and only tiny amounts of carbohydrate, such as a few grains of rice with my duck casserole and a tiny palm-ful of muesli in the mornings.

Initially it was strange to spend an extended period of

time in the company of people, but we are very adaptable animals, and it wasn't long before I was comfortable in the world of people. We have spent many hours sitting by the campfire just talking, and our conversation has ranged across a wide range of topics, including world news and events, mutual friends, hopes and dreams for the future, our dogs, and, of course, they wanted to know all about the mission so I gave them a detailed account of the story so far.

Tomorrow I will be on the march again. I shall set off physically and mentally rejuvenated from my long break here. I had thought it would be a desperate thing to watch the others eat all their luxuries but it hasn't been a problem, due largely to the ducks I guess. It has been great to see Brigitte but subconsciously I've kept my distance from her in some ways, certainly on a physical level.

Brigitte has told me that Greg Serle and Globetag have sponsored Eric Philips and me to attempt the North Pole early next year. Eric and I have worked toward making this expedition a reality since we pioneered a new route to the South Pole in 1998–1999. We had hoped to leave at the end of last year, but were unable to find a sponsor. In other circumstances the news would be very exciting for me, but out here on the mission it has an air of unreality about it. We will leave Australia in mid-February and begin our 1000-kilometre trek from Siberia at the start of March. Whilst this is good news, I had hoped it would happen the following year. If the Great Mission is successful, I will have precious little time between the two expeditions to recover. I file the information away at the back of my mind and forget about it.

DAY 53: SATURDAY, 7 JULY
Warburton Creek

The team has left and Seraphine and I are alone again. The parting was difficult but I managed to stay on top of things. Once on the move, my body felt a bit stiff and weak for the first hour, then suddenly I was on fire – I needed to distract myself from negative thoughts, the emotion of Brigitte's departure and the possibility we won't see each other for two to three months, so I pushed hard and when there was no need to concentrate on navigation, my thoughts turned to the big picture of the route. This all happened in a very positive way and I marched till dark with hardly a stop, covering a lot of ground.

I've reached a new personal milestone today, as this has become my longest solo trip, surpassing Cape York in 1997. I was out for 52 days alone on that one.

DAY 54: SUNDAY, 8 JULY
Warburton Creek

I had another energetic day today and covered a record distance. There were lots of good long runs on flat, smooth claypans with dunes here and there, and a few bits of large, rough gibber to make me earn it!

It was a strange experience to spend three days with the gang after 50 days alone and with the prospect of many more ahead. It was good to switch off from the mission for a while, but at the same time I couldn't shut down completely. As much as possible I attempted to live in the present and forget about the bigger picture, but I could hear the faint rumble of the mission the whole time. That is the sound this trip has – a rumble. The cruiser makes a rumble, changing with different surfaces. My stomach makes a rumble when it wants food, which is most of the time. Finally, I fart a lot. So all things considered, there's a lot of rumbling going on!

Together Brigitte and I spoke of many things: our love, our past, our present, our future, our families and friends, our work and play, our homes and gardens, our chooks and sheep. So now I've got lots to think about. It was warm reassurance that a different but also wonderful life is waiting for me outside the mission, in the not-so-real world. Not-so-real because so often we are surrounded in glass, in concrete and in plastic, living under electric lights. All too often we are involved in activities which alienate us from the natural world, such as staring at a TV or computer screen. We are becoming increasingly removed from the life that humans have lived for most of our history, and the life all other creatures on earth live each day. Of course I have my own share of modern 'madness' to deal with too, but the things I look forward to the most are the ones that bring me closest to the earth: gardening, building a new chook-shed, planting loads of vegetables and hunting. (I've also got a few expeditions to organise and the spring mowing to do, plus clearing and slashing, so I am expecting it to be a busy spring and summer.) By comparison, my massive workload out here is in many ways more under control. Cloaked in routine, it doesn't have the frantic, seemingly out-of-control pace of my 'normal' life.

DAY 55: MONDAY, 9 JULY
Warburton Creek

The Warburton is interesting. Like everywhere else, the conditions and environment here are constantly changing. In terms of travel it is mostly not too bad, but where cattle have been when the ground was soft it is desperately bumpy and slow, with occasional runs of numerous deep craters and holes. Again today I followed bare open claypans at times where the going was very fast. Along the way, I climbed up onto a gibber-summit, which had a wooden 'pyramid' cairn on top. It was quite extraordinary; I've never seen one like it before. It seemed like a good place for a team shot so I set up the self-timer before Seraphine and I took our positions in front of the cairn.

As Malcolm predicted, I haven't seen any people along here and the only chance I will is at the rig road crossing.

The sight on my gun is off from all the jerking on the cart.

The hairline threads that form the aiming cross in the sight are loose. I pulled the sight apart and put a blob of araldite to stabilise the cross. It was very fiddly and I am not sure it is any good. I may have to re-do the thing with cotton, or hair, and glue, which would be extremely difficult. Anyway, I'll have a bit of target practice tomorrow to see whether I've fixed the problem.

This morning my fingers became very numb, even with woollen fingerless gloves on, and it reminded me how easy life is in one's home environment. You press a button for heat! You turn on a tap for water! You flick a switch for light! Not quite the same out here . . .

DAY 56: TUESDAY, 10 JULY
Warburton Creek

Well, there's now a big, black blob inside the sight of my gun, instead of a fine cross. Amazingly it did the trick though, and early this morning I got myself a beautiful duck. I started marching early as it rained a bit from 5 a.m. to 7 a.m. and really looked like it was going to bucket down.

First up I pushed hard to cross a huge, vegetated claypan, before rejoining the creek. The rain was spitting on and off but looked like it could really start pouring a number of times. In the end it held off but the going became more difficult. A number of small tributaries entered the creek, and in one place the gibber of the Sturt Stony Desert came virtually right to the creek's edge for a kilometre or so. The gibber was cut by many small ravines and was very difficult to negotiate. Still, on the whole it was a good run. The next thing to think about is when to cross the Warburton Creek. As usual, there is a lot to take into consideration.

I'd forgotten what bizarre 'blue' light exists of a morning and evening when there are threatening storm clouds about. I love it! Well, just so long as a bucketful of rain doesn't come with it.

On several occasions today I saw a tall mast to the east, which I think is probably on the Birdsville Track. Something to do with communications, I suppose.

I picked up a few gibbers that took my fancy as tomorrow I have the opportunity to stash some stuff. I'll pass a track that is only 10 or 15 kilometres from the Birdsville Track. At the end of the walk, when Brigitte picks me up, we'll drive down and collect the caches I've left along the way. Each time I leave one, I hide it well and make a small map of the area as I plan to leave quite a few behind and it could be difficult to find them in many months time. One place looks very much like another in this kind of country. It really is a huge landscape.

Home life occupies my thoughts when my mind is idle. Not in a negative way, such as pining for what I may be missing, but in a soothing positive way. There are always so many things I want to do back home. Mostly this involves growing more food and producing more meat and animal products.

I am planning a dam, a prospect that excites me a lot. The dam will hold yabbies, fish, water plants and ducks. All that water will have a cooling effect on things, plus it offers swimming, and will attract birds.

Back to the present, and I am sitting in a beautiful camp under a coolabah, overlooking the river and dining on duck. The fall in the land is greater up here and I am certainly going uphill. Every time I saw the river today it was flowing more quickly than it does further downstream. No ducks just here: maybe they prefer spots where the water isn't moving so fast.

DAY 57: WEDNESDAY, 11 JULY
Warburton Creek

It pissed down all night thanks to a full storm with wind, rain, lightning and thunder, which continued into the morning. My guess is that we had about 25 millimetres of rain, or more, and as a result the river level rose about 30 centimetres. The rain has stopped now but the ground is saturated and I am stuck – shit! Déjà vu, anyone? I do the jobs that have needed doing for a while, such as sewing new straps on my hat and watch, and dealing with the gun. The black blob I fixed in the sight was just too big so I have used superglue and hair to make a new cross. I'll sight it in this afternoon and hope that it does the trick. My gun is just so important. Here, now, I wish I had a shotgun. With one easy shot I could kill several, then eat a duck a day for as long as the meat keeps, which is about six to seven days. Still, I've got to do the best I can with what I've got, and I do.

I have been asking the usual questions of the sky: How widespread was the rain? Was it just bad luck, or will something good come of it? At times like this the struggle is purely mental: to stay motivated and optimistic when the situation perhaps doesn't warrant it.

After the river level rose overnight, it went down slightly in the middle of the day and has been rising again since. We crossed the river several times today while trying to catch a duck that I had winged. I have never taught Seraphine how to hunt but she knew exactly what was going on and dived in after the injured bird. The duck couldn't fly but it could still swim and dive, so we chased it for a while, thinking we might tire it out. It kept escaping us and eventually I had to use a second bullet.

The ground around here is very wet and heavy; I may try to escape the floodplain tomorrow and get on sand or gibber, if possible. Whichever way I go will have its problems after a rain like that, and probably for a number of days, even weeks, to come. My feeling is that it was widespread, but how far to the north did it reach? The answer to this question could mean that in the Arunta (Simpson Desert) I might initially get away with carrying only a litre or 3 of water and relying on claypans. As the waterholes were already full, it might not seem a huge saving on what I would have been carrying anyway, but even

7 or so litres makes a difference. I now believe that crossing the Warburton is going to be a big challenge, but we shall cross that bridge when we arrive at the place where it isn't!

I've spent most of today working on bits and pieces, but also thinking of friends and family and remembering the trips we have planned: with my sister and family on the south coast, to rent a cottage, play in the water, go beachcombing, fishing and paddling, and play cards; with my love on deserted islands in the tropics, to live off the fat of the land with a nice drop of coconut milk; with James at Mudawingee and that trip to Mount Wrong; with the old dunes crew to the Coorong. So much to fit in and so little time!

DAY 58: THURSDAY, 12 JULY
Warburton Creek

A curious dingo watched us from the far bank as this morning broke with a heavy fog. An early walk convinced me to stay put for another day: there is simply *too* much mud about and it is impossible to find a route through it. When I returned, the dingo was still there, moving about on the far shore and watching us from different angles. Then, after an hour or so, it just wandered off.

There are Aborigines' grindstones and grinders absolutely everywhere around here. Grindstones are flattish sandstone plates, of anything up to 1 metre in diameter, which are scattered around camp site areas. They have at least one groove worn into them. Aboriginal women collect desert seeds, then, back at their camp, place them in the dish-like groove of a grindstone and pound or grind them with a smaller stone, called a grinder. Here, in the claypans a kilometre from the river, they seem to be every 500 metres. In one area I saw six in the space of a kilometre and a half. They are always clustered in groups, often with a very old, broken-up one and others in better condition. Numerous grinders of all shapes and sizes lie with each grindstone.

Well, today is yet another day of forced rest and all I can do is make the most of it. I have begun to plan my summit push. This is terribly exciting! It is all a long way off but will probably come around sooner than I expect. So, when do I abandon the cruiser? This is a question that will occupy my mind for a long time to come. Obviously I don't want to get it wrong: too early or too late and I could blow the whole thing right at the end. Increasingly, I am thinking I will swap the cruiser for my hauling-harness-cum-backpack at the Donohue Highway. From there it is only 650 kilometres to Burketown, which I could do in three weeks without the cruiser. I'll stew on it a while.

Today I've also started my usual list of things to do when I get home. This is something I seem to do on all long trips. It is a way of grounding myself, of helping me to remember there is more to life than the trip I am on now. The interesting thing about my list is that it's all about Hope. We bought Hope three years ago now. It's a magic place surrounded by forest, in the

Grampians, south of Natimuk. Hope has become my spiritual home and I'd now like to live there full time and only *visit* Natimuk, my social home, not split my time half and half as I had been doing.

These home projects, particularly the ones that take me closer to the earth, such as the vegie patch, the new chook house and run, making compost, etc., are just as important for my balance and harmony as the journeys I embark on. There are so many long-term things to do at Hope, things we shall benefit from and enjoy in the years ahead, and the only way to do them is to live there full-time and get stuck into them. This decision seems so obvious now, but sometimes you need to step away from things to be able to see more clearly. Anyway, it feels good to have reached this point of realisation about my future, and I look forward to my return home all the more because of it.

Tomorrow I should be on the move again. To get here from Wadlarkaninna, where I camped with Brigitte and co., I covered 98 kilometres in four days, which is fantastic going. But with conditions as they are now, I am expecting it to be slow, very, very, slow!

DAY 59: FRIDAY, 13 JULY
near Rig Road crossing, Warburton Creek

Friday the 13th – possibly the hardest day of the trip so far, for just 16.5 kilometres! The terrain was very wet and swampy and

I crossed a system of about 10 or 12 dunes. Several dunes had creeks flowing through them and on one of these creeks was a beautiful little waterhole where I got two ducks. Past the dunes I entered gibber country where I couldn't help but collect a few interesting stones. Then my route took me through a swamp and on to this camp site. I'll leave a stash here as it is only 10 to 12 kilometres from the Birdsville Track. Not surprisingly, what I will leave will be mostly souvenir rocks.

A river crossing here doesn't look good. I'll investigate in the morning. Whenever I do ford the creek, I expect it will take me all day to get everything across, as I want to film the whole thing. It will be an interesting challenge. I'm very tired now as today was hugely demanding. It had its rewards though and I collected two ducks, some beautiful stones and a bag full of native pear. This was my 40th day of travel – gosh, it's a long, hard trip!

DAY 60: SATURDAY, 14 JULY
Warburton Creek, west bank

I am across the occasionally mighty but mostly non-existent Warburton Creek. Where I crossed, the water was about waist deep and I had to carry everything across on my head, one bag at a time. As the pile of gear on 'our' side of the river became smaller, Seraphine became increasingly frantic. I had planned to carry her over as the second last load but she couldn't wait! She swam across, getting swept 10 metres downstream in the process. From the crossing I then marched a couple of kilo-metres to a suitable camp site.

I can't find my head torch anywhere tonight. If I still can't find it tomorrow in the daylight, I may have to go back to where I crossed the creek this morning. It isn't far, but a bit of a waste of time.

DAY 61: SUNDAY, 15 JULY
250 m from last night's camp

'Take as long as it takes, don't worry about it.'

It tried to rain several times in the night, and now it's been rain-ing steadily for about four hours. I did have to go back for my head torch – what a silly error.

The riverbank is a bad place to be if the rain sets in due to the possibility of a big rise in the river level and the potentially solid, sticky clay of the floodout. For those reasons I decided to head west-north-west for the edge of the floodout where it meets the Arunta dune field and sandier soils. (Arunta is the Aboriginal name for the desert that Cecil Madigan named the Simpson Desert in 1929. I have always called it the Arunta.) This was only 10 kilometres away and should have been no problem, but soon after I set off the ground reached that criti-cal point where getting bogged is unavoidable. So I stopped, having travelled a grand total of 250 metres!

116

So, once again the whole mission has seriously stalled. To make the most of this stop, I will collect some nardoo to help my flour situation. Nardoo is a small fern that looks like four-leaf clover. It thrives in this floodout country, covering the ground in many places. The plants produce small pods that can be gathered and pounded between stones. The husks are removed, leaving a yellow flour that is then mixed with water and baked. The whole thing is a slow process, and one I can only contemplate when I am delayed by rain.

I had already collected some good greens and I will go hunting as usual, so things shouldn't be too bad on the food front. For me, being able to accept the forced stop without difficulty is a sign that I have reached a new level of communion with the landscape. I am just another speck of dust moving seemingly randomly with the ebb and flow of the great rhythm of life, no more or less relevant than the myriad other life out here.

This rain is just another test of my patience. Brigitte's words give me strength: 'Take as long as it takes, don't worry about it.' I can't do anything but take as long as it takes, but to not have to worry about the consequences of being home late is a load off my mind. Sometimes one does need to be told.

This is the coldest day of the trip. The wind is icy with rain from the south. I know where that's coming from – Antarctica via the Southern Ocean! This is shaping up to be the slowest week of the trip so far. And there I was thinking the last of my long delays was behind me. Silly duffer. Over the last few nights, the mozzies have been bad for the first time since I started. This is a taste of things to come I imagine, as the further north I move, the more the mozzies and insects are likely to become a problem, particularly when I enter the tropics and approach the Gulf of Carpentaria where there is plenty of water.

What lies ahead, now, I've never seen before. When I walked the Arunta in 1995, it was from the north-west to the centre, not over here on the eastern side. So for me, the country from this point to as far as I get on the mission is all new. A tremendously exciting time lies ahead, as I plunge further into an even broader, ever widening unknown which has no boundaries. But right now, I'm still stuck in the mud!

DAY 62: MONDAY, 16 JULY
same place as last night

I got good drying conditions in the morning, but as the afternoon progressed there were signs of a front coming in from the south-west. Hmm, this looks ominous – more rain? If it doesn't rain tonight, I'll march in the morning, heading straight for the edge of the floodout. Fingers crossed. It looked borderline this evening but with a lot of weaving between puddles and bogs I may just get through.

I finished eating my ducks today and went for a hunt. No joy. This is obviously not prime real estate and water birds of any description are few and far between. Perhaps the creek is flowing too quickly or there are lots of other options for ducks just now, I don't know. Still, I have a good feeling that I shall be getting ducks reasonably regularly for the rest of the trip.

DAY 63: TUESDAY, 17 JULY
southern edge of the Arunta

It was a desperate, slow, laborious job to cross the floodout but now I am on the south side of the Arunta, at the point where the parallel sand ridges, many hundreds of kilometres long, begin. The going will be tough here too, but better than the floodout! The ground is very hummocky, like the country around the Clayton River, on the south side of the Tirari, but I will be better off than before if we have more rain. This is likely, I think, as it threatened all day, today. Not that we need it; there is water everywhere because of the recent succession of good rains.

In the prevailing conditions, my best option seems to be to head north-east, staying as close as possible to the place where the floodout ends and the desert begins. Here I should find sandier soils and less mud. If so, I'll continue on this line for 60 to 80 kilometres and then head north-north-west into the Arunta up the Eyre Creek.

I saw many dingoes today, mostly in pairs. Usually Seraphine doesn't see them and their scent doesn't interest her at all, which is just fine by me. They are trouble where she is concerned. Also of danger to her are birds of prey. She is a very small dog and is vulnerable to aerial attack. The wedge-tailed eagle, Australia's largest bird of prey, is common out here and capable of taking young lambs, so I don't imagine one would have a problem picking up Seraphine! Sometimes they hover over her and I call her in – 'stay close' is a command she understands all too well.

A very weary Jon tonight!

'Je t'aime, my freckly man!'

DAY 64: WEDNESDAY, 18 JULY
southern edge of the Arunta

Wow, what a swamp I got caught in today, as well as having to negotiate the most wicked terrain of the trip so far: hummocky mud with dense, borderline vegetation. Just 1 kilometre of this took me 2 hours and a massive amount of energy. It was more difficult than anticipated, and at times extreme, but fortunately I'd seen it coming and was already thinking that covering 12 to 18 kilometres a day would be something to feel good about. I'd better scale that down again; just as well I estimated the second third of the mission to be as slow as the first.

A herd of about 10 or 12 camels loitered about 1 kilometre from our camp until dusk. Earlier today in the marsh I crossed two fences, each running north-east. On this side there are only camel pad prints, so it would seem there are no cattle in this area. This is good for me because when cattle walk over heavy, wet ground, they leave deep holes that, when dry, create terribly, bumpy areas that make for some of the hardest travel.

Wherever I look I see signs of the long, nomadic Aboriginal occupation of the land. In the dry country that I am traversing now, they come mostly in the form of grindstones.

DAY 65: THURSDAY, 19 JULY
southern edge of the Arunta

There is a lake-like area (though no lake is marked on my map) with a squillion birds just to my north! The number of birds of all descriptions is staggering. So is the amount of water about. The ground is saturated with it and covered with thick new growth – desperate stuff to get through. Which route will be best? What is the best point to enter Eyre Creek? I can head north to join the creek anytime over the next 35 kilometres. The main channel of the Eyre Creek ends in large areas of floodout. Should I try here, somewhere in the middle or over on the east side? Not here, I think – it has to be better somewhere else. This heavy going is seriously sapping my strength, and taking the right route up to join the Eyre Creek could be crucial. Like a lot of things, I've got to make it up as I go, on the run so to speak.

I saw a dozen camels at close quarters today. Unfortunately they bolted when I got out of my harness to shoot some film. There were several young ones and a massive bull. They quickly herded into a circle when they saw me and then headed off with Mr Bull in the rear. They really were a magnificent sight.

DAY 66: THURSDAY, 20 JULY
Tepaminkanie Waterhole

A huge, desperate day with only 11.5 kilometres to show for it – this is not on. Perhaps the east side of the Eyre Creek floodout is best. It appears on the map that there may be less swampy ground there. My fingers are tightly crossed that this wet, heavily vegetated country is only on the floodout as far as the dunes. If the current conditions are what I can expect for a few hundred kilometres or more, then I can see myself using too much energy for too little distance, and the mission will be in jeopardy. I have decided to ease off a little until I see what the ground is like at the eastern entry point of Eyre Creek. The plan is to do some hunting and not overdo things generally as the conditions may soon improve.

Many times today I became bogged and had to unload half my gear to free the cruiser. Somehow I managed to keep my cool, though I did catch myself saying out loud that this was my choice, my trip, my dream, and my reality, and that getting agro or negative was a ridiculous waste of energy that would be better directed in a positive fashion to get on with the simple task at hand. It has been a very, very taxing day, and I am feeling drained.

I got two ducks today, which will help boost my energy levels. One was in a pool behind last night's camp and the other in the channel leading into the waterhole where I am now. I need to eat more ducks along the way – preferably the bigger ones!

DAY 67: FRIDAY, 21 JULY
Tepaminkanie Waterhole – still

The plan for today was simple; cross this watercourse and the next, 1.5 kilometres from here, then call it quits. So I had a mostly leisurely morning, busying myself with the many small jobs that always need doing. I then packed up and went on reconnaissance without the cruiser. Lucky I did; it turned out that the route I had planned involved five channel crossings in the next 500 metres, each 10 to 20 metres across from firm ground to firm ground. All of them had ankle-deep, soft mud and water up to waist high, and I would have had to unload and ferry everything across, five times in a row. There had to be a better way and the next best I could find involved two crossings, 300 metres apart, with, presumably, one more at the next waterhole. A much better option.

The first of these dreaded crossings is right in front of last night's camp, but my recce took a long time and my body called for a break. I decided to make the crossing in the morning. It was the best move, really, as the past few days have taken a terrible toll and I needed to regain my energy, and think of the best strategy to overcome my situation. It's been a valuable day actually. I seem to have made a slight mental shift as I realise I have to take this extremely difficult stretch in a more relaxed fashion.

Tomorrow I shall progress slowly and safely. These bogs and the incredibly bumpy surface of the floodout mean injury is never far away. I try not to overdo it physically, and mentally I don't let a lack of good progress get me down. Things will improve and until they do, husband your strength, Jon, and don't hurl it all at any one difficult stretch.

DAY 68: SATURDAY, 22 JULY
half way between Tepaminkanie and Burt waterholes

Today I came about 8 or 10 kilometres in 9 hours. I usually only count the time spent actually walking, but today there were so many breaks I didn't bother!

During the course of the day, I waded across a waterhole and five channels. These innocuous-looking channels are sometimes just 2 metres across, but it is impossible to get the laden cruiser through them without sinking to lower-calf in the mud. When that happens, the cruiser tilts forward and the leading edge acts like a plough. Well, more like an anchor, really! Therefore, each crossing requires me to carry four loads across, the last being the cruiser itself. It all takes a long time and lots of energy but I hardly looked at my watch and did everything at a slow pace, which seemed to work. The difference between pushing hard or taking it slowly is only about 1 or 2 kilometres in these conditions. I need far less food (fuel) too, if I take it easy.

I am desperately hoping to see better conditions later tomorrow as I approach the east side of the Eyre Creek flood-out where it merges with Goyder Lagoon. Perhaps I should spend a day doing a big recce before committing myself to following the creek. I'm wondering whether terrain conditions will push me even further east into the narrow strip between Eyre Creek and the desert's east boundary where there is no creek. No water source is a problem.

Hopefully it will all fall into place but for the moment it is hard to imagine that this mission can possibly succeed. I need to keep telling myself that I'm a long way from being out of the race yet, and perhaps in just a day or three this struggle will be replaced by a new optimism as I take off again at a rate of knots. This difficult stretch is testing my resilience. There is a huge amount of fat in the duck I shot today and God knows we need it. My body has already lost a massive amount of weight – I'd guess about 12 to 15 kilograms – and while not yet thin, I'm decidedly lean! Seraphine just seems to get more muscular as the weeks go by and my guess is that she is actually a little heavier than when we started. So, with almost-full bellies tonight, the team is happy. Happy with the new moon too.

Somewhere around here I have crossed Captain Charles Sturt's tracks from his 1844–46 expedition. His team was the first group of Europeans to plunge deep into Australia's driest region. Sturt's objective was to reach the centre of the continent, where many believed lay an inland sea. The expedition carried a boat from Adelaide, abandoning it only when the endless sand ridges of the Strzelecki Desert proved too difficult for the bullock carts. At that point, near the adjoining borders of Queensland, New South Wales and South Australia, Sturt established a base camp from which two lightweight pushes were made to try to reach the centre. Both were stopped by the massive sand ridges of the Arunta and a desperate shortage of water. Sturt pushed his whole team to the limits of human endurance, demonstrating on many occasions an uncanny ability to know just when to retreat; a day or two earlier and the men would not have given their best, a day or two later and they would not have survived. I will be following Sturt's route over the next few hundred kilometres.

DAY 69: SUNDAY, 23 JULY
Burt Waterhole

Another desperate day, but there was a little room for optimism when the going improved towards the end. Despite taking it easy I am feeling done in and am wondering if this is cause for concern. Am I going downhill and weakening before reaching the halfway point? I will have been out here for 70 days tomorrow, so I guess it is possible. I do need a decent rest and perhaps a few days here will restore my balance and focus, which have taken a battering over the past two weeks.

A rest will also give me much needed time to cross a few things off my growing to-do list:

Fix Seraphine's coat	Clean gun
Sort food	Clean cameras
Pull out 'summit' rations	Clean me
Fish, hunt	Leave depot
Wash clothes	REST!
Study maps	Fix pants
Clean clothes	

DAY 70: MONDAY, 24 JULY
Burt Waterhole

Happy birthday to Dad and to Vero! She might be Brigitte's sister, but I consider her my sister too!

What a busy day it has been. I studied the maps from

here across the Arunta to the Donohue Highway and I feel like the whole thing hangs in the balance. I looked carefully at the story so far, including the maps and log and I feel more confident. Perhaps the days of longer distance, from the Oodnadatta Track to halfway along the Warburton Creek, were too much. From previous trips I knew I could march at that pace, but maybe it is too draining to sustain on the much longer and much harder Great Mission. In the terrain and conditions of the past while, it has been impossible to maintain the average speed I had hoped for. But even when the route becomes easier, perhaps I shouldn't be trying to march 24 to 27 kilometres per day. Maybe I should be content with less. I don't know, but I do know that only the correct strategy and tactics will get me through. I must make the correct decision every time.

When I summitted Everest alone, breaking trail the whole way through ankle- to chest-deep snow, I felt tired at the end but had plenty of energy in reserve. At the end of most days on the Great Mission, I am worn out, exhausted, and struggling to make camp, drawing heavily on willpower to get everything done.

This waterhole is just beautiful! It is sandwiched between two eroded dunes and is full to the brim, like all the waterholes so far except those at the start. It is right where the floodout ends and the dunes begin and behind it is a large, open, flat swale that feeds the waterhole. This is unusual and is marked on the map, along with several others along here, as having no vegetation. I suspect that on occasions the whole area becomes a large, shallow lake, drowning all growth.

As I sit here by this lovely shore, my thoughts wander to Wollongong and the birthday celebration there. It would also have been Nanna's birthday if she were still alive. How old would she be now?

That was a short wander; I am back to thinking about the mission. I do hope to be able to push hard again on this walk. I imagine it will happen when I abandon the cruiser and set off on my summit push. But where will that be? At present I still think it's highly likely that when I reach the Donohue Highway, 500 kilometres from here, I'll have no choice but to go for it. But to ensure I have enough in reserve for the push, perhaps I will take it slower from here to the highway.

It seriously threatened to rain all this afternoon and into the evening, but now the weather seems to be clearing up. It's incredible how one's outlook can swing from day to day. The important thing is not to overreact to the current circumstances and to keep an eye on the big picture with a level head. I suppose in some ways this is at the core of survival.

'Thinking of you . . . and our next challenge together.'

Ditto. So long as it's a small, short, friendly one!

DAY 71: TUESDAY, 25 JULY
Burt Waterhole

Today was another busy day although I actually managed to lie in till 9.30 a.m. I was awake from first light, but I stayed in bed and it was good to rest. My bowels are a little loose just now. Is it the water?

I have bundled a few things together to leave here. The Birdsville Inside Track is closed at the moment, but it passes close by here and might be open by the time this walk is over. Going through everything was a worthwhile exercise and I did come across a few things I had forgotten about or didn't know I had, like my hairbrush and half a candle from the start. I don't think I need either! I am also leaving the desalinator; it is heavy, and there is so much fresh water about that I might not need it again. Still, it was a difficult decision.

I also checked over my food stores. I definitely can't leave any of them behind; I'll be lucky if I have enough to finish the mission. My rations are pretty low, but I'll just have to make do. The more bush tucker I find along the way, the longer my stores will last. It is hard to know just how long I can string them out.

From now on I head north into the Arunta, and, just as before a big climb, there are a few butterflies in my stomach. When I leave here, I will start on the longest remote stretch of the walk. An emergency escape from the desert would be difficult, as I'd have to walk up and over endless parallel sand ridges.

My head swims with many questions which will only be answered along the way. My biggest fear is that it will all be marshy swamp. If it is, what do I do? Retreat back here and travel a little more east-north-east? Press on regardless? Being on the cusp of this new phase of the trip is an exhilarating feeling that I haven't experienced so strongly since the start of the Great Mission. The Arunta is a big place and a lot of the time I shall be a long way from towns, roads, farms and people until I reach the Donohue Highway to the desert's north.

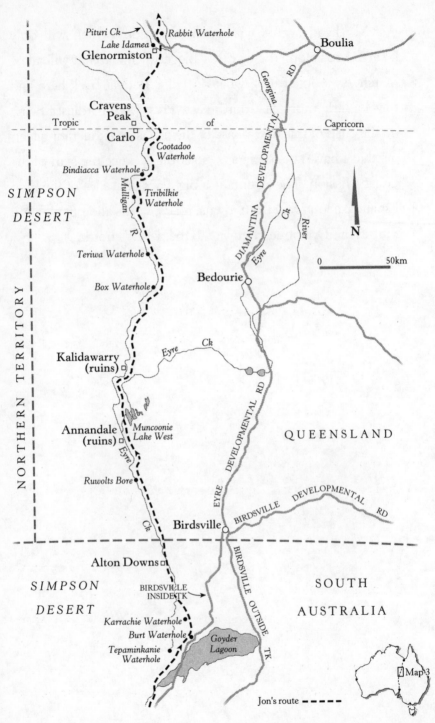

Pituri Ck → • *Rabbit Waterhole*
Lake Idamea •
Glenormiston □

Boulia ◉

Cravens Peak □

Tropic □ of □ Capricorn
Carlo •
Cootadoo Waterhole

SIMPSON
DESERT

Bindiacca Waterhole •
Tiribilkie Waterhole •

Mulligan R

Teriwa Waterhole •

N

Box Waterhole •

Bedourie ◉

Eyre Ck

Kalidawarry (ruins) □

0 ___ 50km

N
O
R
T
H
E
R
N

T
E
R
R
I
T
O
R
Y

Annandale (ruins) □
Muncoonie Lake West

Eyre

QUEENSLAND

Ruwolts Bore •

EYRE DEVELOPMENTAL RD

DIAMANTINA DEVELOPMENTAL

Georgina RD

Eyre Ck

River

BIRDSVILLE DEVELOPMENTAL RD

Ck

Birdsville ◉

BIRDSVILLE OUTSIDE TK

Alton Downs □

BIRDSVILLE INSIDE TK →

SOUTH

SIMPSON
DESERT

Karrachie Waterhole •
Burt Waterhole •
Tepaminkanie Waterhole •

Goyder Lagoon

AUSTRALIA

Jon's route ▬ ▬ ▬

Map 3

MAP 3: EYRE CREEK TO GLENORMISTON

6

THE EYRE CREEK

A New Beginning

DAY 72: WEDNESDAY, 26 JULY
Karrachie Waterhole

Stage Six has begun well. Stage Six is Eyre Creek to the Muncoonie lakes or thereabouts. The whole thing is roughly 200 kilometres of the Arunta, and I've taken it easy for the first 15. I promised myself I would. I could have done more but I don't want to fall into the usual trap of doing too much after a rest day. That could easily happen; the conditions are pretty good. Pace yourself, Jon.

Initially I went through some dunes very much like those in the Tirari, then across open country that is typical of these parts. In places the vegetation is a bit thick. There is a lot of new growth from good rains but so far no bog or marsh. Fingers crossed it stays that way.

I am camped at another waterhole with scarred trees and

grindstones. Scarred trees can be seen across the continent. The scars are the result of pieces of wood or bark being removed by the Aboriginal people, who use them to make anything from dishes and spear throwers to canoes. They are commonly found near water.

I shot what I hope is some good film this morning as I passed across an incredible flat field of yellow flowers. I had seen this type of field earlier in the mission, when I approached Burt Waterhole, but was too tired to film then. This time, there was so much pollen that my boots and gaiters and Seraphine's feet turned yellow. In the early morning light it was sensational.

One of my teeth is falling apart. A bit came away yesterday. And just now, as I cleaned my teeth, another bit fell away. I initially thought it was a bit of old filling, but in fact it is a bit of tooth. This concerns me greatly, of course. I've always known that tooth trouble is perhaps the most likely physical problem that would stop me. It has come very close to ending several of my previous expeditions; my teeth are in terrible shape. It is hard not to get a bit of grit in your dinner when you live in the dirt, so you have to be especially careful. I have cloves and clove oil in my first aid kit; they are both good local anaesthetics for mouth problems. There's nothing I can do but keep my teeth clean and hope for the best.

DAY 73: THURSDAY, 27 JULY
in the Arunta somewhere

Today was a great day, with a bit of everything thrown in. It began when I left the waterhole and saw an edge-ground axe head made of polished stone. It was the first time I'd ever come across such a tool so it was very exciting and, as often happens, it set me thinking of the ancestors who first inhabited this land. They were completely in tune with the rhythms of life around them, having lived here continuously for tens of thousands of years.

There is not much happening in this neck of the woods. Although it is farmed, I've seen no cattle, fences or tracks yet. I know I will sooner or later, but things are few and far between and the region has a deliciously isolated feel.

Today I crossed a marshy area not marked on the map, and came upon a number of small waterholes that I think fill from drainage off the long clay slopes at the base of the dunes. I crossed four dunes and in between them were some good runs on flat, level ground with only a bit of weaving. Oh, and there were some hideously tight patches of lignum, a chaotic vine-like bush that can sometimes be impossible to negotiate. So far it seems that as long as I'm prepared to cross dunes occasionally, the route is mostly good.

It feels to me like it has been a big day, although I'm not sure exactly how far I've come. I am in an area of the desert with no distinctive geographical features, and both my pace and course have been erratic. This makes it difficult to work out the distance covered as I usually multiply my kilometres per hour by the hours marched. Tomorrow I am aiming to be camped at the main channel of the Eyre Creek, and from there I can work backwards to figure out my distances.

It is incredible to be walking across a continent. Well, trying to, anyway. That's what's important, having a go. On my first three attempts at the mission I never felt I had the chance to give it my best shot. This time around I have, and I will accept the outcome, regardless of how much further I get, with deep satisfaction. The attempt is everything, the outcome relatively irrelevant.

I really am just slowly crawling across! Although I have now been out here for 73 days, the excitement of it all remains as fresh as on day one. It is an exhilarating feeling and it gives me great strength and motivation. This journey was a big dream for me, and in certain ways it is as dreamy to be living it as it was to dream about it. I'll often think back on this in the years and decades ahead. To be so alone in such a big empty space *is* bordering on a dream.

DAY 74: FRIDAY, 28 JULY
near Alton Downs

What a long hard day – I am very tired. I have covered about 40 kilometres in the last two days; that's not bad. The floodout here is almost dry but in places it's heavily vegetated with cane grass, lignum, saltbush and something similar. In other areas there is incredibly lush green growth, the sort you would never expect to see in the desert: three-metre high, soft-stemmed, luxuriant, green flowering plants. I'll film some this evening.

For the first time I am camped on the Eyre Creek main channel. I'm not sure whether it is flowing here, if so it's very slow. There is water as far as I can see in both directions. Early to bed for the Muir-Snupesen team. Tomorrow night we should be in Queensland!

DAY 75: SATURDAY, 29 JULY
a distributary of Eyre Creek

Day 75 and I've had just 50 full walking days and 25 stationary ones. Of the 'rest' days I think only six were voluntary. Anyway, I made it to Queensland in one piece and there was good hunting on the way. I shot three ducks: one in the early morning, one on the march at Terrachi Waterhole and one on arrival here.

I discovered just how effective my 'fridge' is the other day. When I woke up, my tarp was covered in a film of ice that I put in the fridge – on the shafts under my down sleeping bags and sleeping mat. It was a nice sunny day and yet when I unpacked in the evening, the ice was still there! I already knew that I could keep meat for seven or eight days, but this was a good demonstration of how well the system works.

I also picked some Ulcardo melons, which I had never had before. They are small (2 to 5 centimetres long), green, oval fruits that contain lots of slender seeds in a watery pulp. They are yummy, taste like baby cucumbers and there are loads of them. Also on the menu today: bloated bovine! I had heard from several sources that it was well worth trying so when I came across a dead cow today I was more than keen. The cow had been dead for a week or so and parts of it were crawling with maggots. As I cut into the rump, a continuous deflating sound, very similar to a fart, emerged from its bum. The smell was as one could imagine, but it would have taken more than that to turn me off – I am that hungry! The meat tasted like steak that needs to be eaten and I thoroughly enjoyed it.

Finally, I'm off 'conglomerate map 5!' This is one of the photocopied maps that are each made up of two or three 1/250 000 maps stuck together in one long strip, and number 5 has taken an eternity.

DAY 76: SUNDAY, 30 JULY
near Ruwolts Bore

Today I saw people. On my route I hit the QAA line, an old seismic survey line that is now the four-wheel-drive tourist route across the Simpson Desert, and I followed it hoping to see someone and get a message out. There were fresh tyre tracks and with the creek trickling I figured the road must be open, and that sooner or later I'd bump into cars. Well I did: three vehicles, with occupants who were rather perplexed by the sight of us. They all stopped and we had a yarn. It had been three and a half weeks since I had seen anyone and it was very strange to suddenly be social again. They had recently driven past Peter Treseder and Tim Jarvis, two desert walkers who were nearing the end of their Great Victoria Desert crossing. Anyway, the four-wheel-drive mob will now be in Birdsville. I asked one of them, Geoff Simpson, to call Brigitte and tell her we reached the junction of the QAA line and Eyre Creek on 30 July, and that Seraphine and I were both doing well.

This has been my most productive day yet but that's not hard when you are on a vehicle track for most of the day. I am looking forward to leaving it behind tomorrow; I find following roads boring and not much of a challenge.

It is getting warmer. This is to be expected though, as I'm heading north and soon I'll be in the tropics! I haven't been to the tropics since the 'Encounters' trip in 1997, when I paddled solo from Cooktown to the tip of Cape York, the northern-most point of Australia. I must get back to the Queensland coast in a kayak; it is always such a beautiful adventure. After time spent in the desert I dream of such places. And after time amongst the deserted islands and coast of far north Queensland, I dream of the desert. Such is life.

DAY 77: MONDAY, 31 JULY
the Arunta

I have just had a very hard day for a gain of 18 kilometres as the crow flies. I crossed several massive dunes, which was very slow and very demanding but I kept away from the Eyre Creek as several floodout creeks come this way and it would have been even slower. It should be okay to rejoin it in the morning, though, and according to the map I'll have an uninterrupted run up to the Muncoonie lakes.

It has been hot and today for the first time on the trip I needed a little lie down during the day. I was really feeling a bit weak all day, and I am crossing my fingers that it is not the beginning of the end.

I made a late start as I had to cross over a dune to pick up 10 litres of water from Eyre Creek. The water and the two ducks I caught meant an extra load all of a sudden and perhaps that was part of my problem today. Anyway, tomorrow I'll be back by the water and I've just eaten a duck so the cruiser will be a little lighter.

I just had a dingo scare! All of a sudden three of them were 10 metres or so from me, seemingly unaware of my presence. Seraphine saw them a moment after I did, and I grabbed the gun and we both made a racket – me yelling, Seraphine barking – running towards the dingoes. They did retreat but soon Seraphine was between two of them. They started closing in so I fired and got one, which ran off yelping. I'm not sure where I got it, but probably somewhere non-critical judging from its behaviour. The other two also fled. It was a close call for Seraphine and the episode left me slightly shaken. Seraphine is very courageous and fearless and it could easily get her badly wounded, or even killed where packs of dingoes are concerned.

We are now approaching the halfway mark of the mission in kilometres marched. Everything now comes down to arriving at the north side of the desert, at the Donohue Highway, with enough energy and food for a dash to Burketown over the final third of the continent. Though I'm quietly confident, as always, it is a hell of a way and the mission is far from in the bag. This evening's visitors have left me wondering how many bullets to put away for emergencies should I start to run out. Two? Five? It looks like I should have brought another 25 or so.

DAY 78: TUESDAY, 1 AUGUST
Annandale Ruins, Annandale Waterhole

'Deserts, white and red, space, blue sky, white sun, my love.'

I feel more than ever before in my life that I have simply melted into the landscape. It was an easy route to follow the swale down to the creek and then along the creek itself, and I moved much better and arrived here early. Despite the mostly good going and though I feel better than yesterday, I am still somehow weak, particularly in the thighs. The massive effort of

141

making it halfway is really beginning to take a toll. So I decided to stop, and have spent the afternoon fixing clothes and boots, cleaning things, charging batteries and doing a lot of filming of birds and ruins. There is lots of very old and rusted farming machinery lying around what is left of the homestead – a few crumbling walls and a proud chimney.

Somewhere close to here, Sturt was forced to retreat from his audacious attempt to reach Australia's centre. Way out on a limb and experiencing much drier conditions than those prevailing now, he wrote to his wife:

Sunday, 7 September 1845

Ascending one of the sand ridges I saw a numberless succession of these terrific objects rising above each other to the E and W. Northwards, they ran before me for more than 15 miles . . . The scene was awfully fearful, dear Charlotte. A kind of dread came over me as I gazed upon it. It looked like the entrance into hell. Mr Browne stood horrified. 'Did man,' he exclaimed, 'ever see such a place?'

Edward Stokes, To the Inland Sea, Century Hutchinson, Melbourne,
1984, p. 182.

DAY 79: WEDNESDAY, 2 AUGUST
Muncoonie Lake West

Wow, this place is incredible. It looks a bit like Coongie Lake in South Australia, like a jewel in the desert.

It was a tough haul to get here, though. Rounding the ends of dunes that butted into the creek was hard work and generally the ground is sandier. I also climbed over a monster dune to get here.

The dunes are getting redder, which happens the further north in the desert you go. The sand originates in country south of the desert, has a high clay content and is pale or white. As the prevailing winds slowly move them north-north-west, the clay particles weather and iron oxide is released, coating the sand with a red crust. The oldest and reddest sands are found in the desert's north.

Things seem to be going along well after my battle with the Warburton, though it would be nice to be able to pick up the pace a bit. My body felt fine today. I guess I had just pushed too hard a couple of days back.

The bloated bovine has been great! It is always good to have a change and though there is not as much fat on it as on the ducks, it's going down well nevertheless.

DAY 80: THURSDAY, 3 AUGUST
a channel north of the Muncoonie lakes

What a day! I've covered 25 kilometres over the ground to come just 15.5 kilometres as the crow flies. My line squiggled all over the place because of water, marsh and vegetation.

The day started with the crossing of a minor flowing

channel. That was fine; the banks and the bottom were solid and the water not too deep. A bit later, while crossing an area between a channel and a dune, I noticed a dust cloud about 4 kilometres away in the direction I was headed. At first I thought it was a willy willy but it stayed pretty stationary. As I finally approached I saw a big mob of cattle being mustered. People! Did I want to meet them? The going on the swale between us looked impossible and the base of the dune looked much better, but then I would be on a collision course with the musterers. I stopped and had a break at the same time they did. It was the middle of a hot day and the cattle must have needed to rest.

I decided I may as well get going round the base of the dune, and when I came out of the vegetation, which was waist-to-chest high, the boss saw me and came straight over. Soon all six of them and I were chatting away. They were amazed to see someone walking out here and the mission itself blew them away. One of them had seen my tracks about 50 kilometres or more south. As we were talking, someone came in on the radio. (The musterers wear them strapped to their chest.) It was their helicopter pilot, wanting to know what was going on. 'We're just talking to someone who is walking,' they radioed back. Five minutes later, the helicopter, which helps with the mustering, was overhead – the pilot thought they were joking!

I scored three cigarettes and they filled in a form saying they had not assisted me, other than posting a letter and giving me three smokes. I promised them a postcard from

Burketown or as far as I get. It was good to have a chat with these Aboriginal stockmen who know and understand the land so well, and so can grasp the enormity of my challenge.

Not long after saying goodbye, I scored my second bloated bovine. This one was obviously the victim of the muster and heat. I stocked up on steaks and kept going.

I have not crossed a single fence in a number of days now, though I've seen a few remains.

As I walked along, I remembered the words of one of the lads, 'So you're really out here alone? I mean, there's no support vehicle or anything like that around?'

7

THE MULLIGAN RIVER

Just Keep Walking

DAY 81: FRIDAY, 4 AUGUST
Kalidawarry Ruins, Mulligan River

I'm officially just over halfway! The second half will fly by, I'm sure of it. Also, Stage Six, the Eyre Creek, is over and Stage Seven, the Mulligan River, begins here. The Mulligan River originates 300 kilometres north of here at the north-eastern margin of the desert, and flows into Eyre Creek just south of my current position. The river is very wide where I am now. It's probably about 100 metres across and looks full, but although I can't be sure, I don't think it is flowing. If it *is* flowing, my supply of fresh water is guaranteed over the next 200 kilometres. If not, the smaller waterholes will soon turn to salt, forcing me to carry more water.

I had an easy start today on good, relatively open clay followed by a desperate finish on hummocky sand with tiny ridges up to 4 metres high. I'm very tired now. Last night I didn't get to sleep until after 1 a.m. and I slept through the alarm. So, a late start, a late and hot finish, and hardly enough energy to write.

Something Malcolm Mitchell said to me way down south in Muloorina keeps playing around in my mind, 'You'll complete your walk this time – just keep walking.' Just keep walking – that's all I really need to do – just keep walking, just keep walking . . .

An important point to finish on, though; my boots are wearing out. In one spot, on the right heel, the hard rubber sole has worn through to expose a softer, spongier layer. If these boots fall apart, I am in deep trouble and I must come up with some sort of solution to keep them going. Over the past few years I've been wearing the same model boot and am surprised to see them wearing through after just 1300 kilometres.

DAY 82: SATURDAY, 5 AUGUST
Mulligan River

It has been a long hard day but I enjoyed the struggle. For about 3 or 4 kilometres towards the end I encountered flat, open clay country and was able to get in top gear and fly for a bit. It was a welcome change from the slow, sandy, hummocky stuff that I had been in for most of the day.

I wake up at 5.35 a.m. at the moment, and it is light enough to walk at 6.20 a.m. now, as opposed to 6.40 a.m. on the shortest days of the walk. It is also getting warmer, and for the first time on the trip I am shirtless well after dark.

Because of this change in temperature there are a few things I'd like to get rid of now, like my second, heavier sleeping bag. Recently I have been using my light sleeping bag, and even that only in the cooler hours before I get up. The problem is that there is nowhere to leave it, and I simply can't throw good things away. I'll wait and stash them under a bush when I reach the Donohue Highway, then Brigitte and I can pick them up on the drive home from Burketown.

Today I thought about my love a lot and it lent me a special strength and vitality of mind, body and spirit. It will be time for lots of shared moments by journey's end.

Despite the day-by-day trials and tribulations, it suddenly seems like I am flying along. Since the stall mid-Warburton and my fresh start up Eyre Creek I have been faster. The cruiser is now 35 to 38 kilograms lighter in food and equipment than on departure and I sometimes think I'm only now starting to notice it. Also, the conditions have been mostly good since leaving the Warburton; I haven't had a day off and mentally I did begin anew after the loss of momentum caused by the heavy rains. Still, who knows what lies just ahead. A major setback could easily occur.

The initial wide expanse of the creek has given way to more of a gutter here at tonight's camp site, with not so many trees about and salt deposits lining the banks. The water is ever so slightly salty and quite shallow. Though the river is not flowing, it does seem to be a continuous body of water here.

It is nice to have the moon full again. Just one more and the mission will be over.

DAY 83: SUNDAY, 6 AUGUST
Mulligan River

So far the river is treating me well and the going is very good. As I traversed the shore of Lake Torquinie today, I passed by what must have been tens of thousands of dead fish. They were all dried out and some had good bits of sun-dried meat that I stripped off and put in my tucker bag. When floods come down these rivers the fish get washed out of their sanctuaries in the permanent waterholes and into huge floodout areas. At the same time there is a population explosion as the floods carry nutrients downstream. When the floodwaters subside, the fish die off in their millions.

I had a shorter day today as I slowed down a bit and did a lot of filming. I have been slightly obsessed with progress since starting up Eyre Creek, and perhaps this is at the cost of other things that are also important. A stocktake revealed that I still have enough food to see me through (just), about 19 kilograms out of the 46 I started with, and can afford to try to get more footage.

Today I saw some amazing artefacts: a beautiful heavy edge-ground chopper and also a cute little grindstone with a dish just 5 centimetres across and perfectly round.

DAY 84: MONDAY, 7 AUGUST
near Box Waterhole, Mulligan River

> *'I look at the moon in the sky and I think of you.*
> *I smile at the moon in the sky and you are with me.'*

I do the same.

Camels are mingling with cattle by the waterhole I'm currently camped at. Well, waterhole is not the right word, shitty little puddle would be more appropriate. Still, it's the only one going.

It somehow seems like today was long and hard. Huge samphire flats, sometimes hummocky like the ones around the Wimmera salt lakes in Victoria, are the kind of country I am often crossing just now, with the massive dunes of the Arunta to my right and left. Samphire is a succulent plant that forms extensive mats up to 30 centimetres high on salty ground. Though edible, it is a last-resort green as its flavour is poor, and it tends to be very salty. I also crossed a fence today; I imagine they will start to become more frequent as I approach the desert's edge.

A few days back I suddenly had the feeling the trip was drawing to a close. Why I had that impression I can't figure out, given that I've only just crossed the halfway mark. I am very tired and falling asleep as I write. It is 8 p.m. and I have been at it non-stop – packing, unpacking, walking, cooking, etc. – since 5.30 a.m., just like every other day. Today was Day 84, that's exactly how long it took us to establish a new route to the South

Pole. So, as of tomorrow, this will be my longest walk. It will be a few more days before it becomes the furthest.

DAY 85: TUESDAY, 8 AUGUST
Teriwa Waterhole, Mulligan River

I had a good run today on saltbush and samphire claypans, though of course there were some hard bits. That was after another terrible night, lying awake till about 2.30 a.m.

I passed by a lovely big waterhole on the river bend en route and shot a duck. The steaks from bloated bovine no. 2 will be finished tonight.

I have been giving a lot of thought to the route ahead as at some point on the next map I have got to decide which direction to take for the following 200 kilometres. I am now looking at three options. The far-west route involves the longest waterless sections and this would mean a slow finish to the mission. The mid-west, or middle, is the next most difficult. Both these routes would be slower and more physically demanding and I am concerned that by making it unnecessarily harder for myself, I increase the chances of blowing it. While this is a risk I have been taking since the start, instinct tells me to take the easiest, surest route. This is the east route and by taking it I will still cover the same final 400 kilometres: the top of the Georgina River across the Barkly Tableland, the O'Shanassy River into the Gregory River and the Gregory into the Gulf of Carpentaria. It would just mean hooking into the Georgina earlier and following it up. This still avoids the whole area around Mount Isa, which is on the most direct line from here to Burketown; I don't want to walk through populated country. One of the problems with my proposed east route is that I would be 'off map' for 160 kilometres or so. This could be fun, but it does make the 'easier' option more difficult than it would otherwise be. Before I decide which option to choose, I need to study my maps a bit more and think it all through. That's plenty to stew over on the march for the next week to 10 days!

DAY 86: WEDNESDAY, 9 AUGUST
Tiribilkie Waterhole, Mulligan River

This morning was desperately slow. I slept 15 minutes past the alarm and when I finally got going I really struggled for the first 2 hours.

The dunes are getting very red now, a sign that I am nearing the top of the desert.

When I see a fence, a track, cattle, really anything to do with farming, I think of Hope. My plans, hopes and dreams are there.

I have found a magic stone. It's a meteorite; a rock from another world. At least, I think that's what it is.

I had another big look at the maps today and calculated the distance to Burketown: 830 kilometres. Maybe the trip *is* coming to an end if I do 30 kilometres per day for the last 600 kilometres. But can I? Carrying just a pack should make it possible to speed up and I have to think very carefully about where I will abandon the cruiser. I will put everything I need for the summit push together and see how the pack feels. This will help me decide.

DAY 87: THURSDAY, 10 AUGUST
Bindiacca Waterhole, Mulligan River

The day got off to a bad start when Seraphine scared off some ducks I was stalking just after setting off. I also saw another herd of camels on the march, and a really odd-looking thing ran off as I approached this waterhole. It really threw me as I have no idea what it was. A cross between a koala and a hare, I'd say! Or was it a feral cat without a tail?

It is amazing just how many grindstone shards there are about. Every claypan and every dune anywhere near a watercourse has dozens. Earlier on I saw a cute little 'pebble' grindstone.

Again today, after negotiating a rocky hill from last night's waterhole, I crossed more samphire flats right up to the very large Pulchera Waterhole. I then cut a corner and had to negotiate some tight spinifex before crossing a mixed bag of terrain to get here. I also crossed a track, which was the closest to a road I've seen in a long time. Overall it was pretty slow going.

This waterhole has the freshest water since Eyre Creek. That's because it's not on the main channel, but rather is 'back filled' when the river floods.

It has been cold these last few nights and I am glad I still have two sleeping bags. Yesterday, after studying the maps, I began a new column in my log: distance remaining. Including this right from the start would have been too disheartening. Now, as I am past halfway and approaching the final push, it is a positive spur. The distance is 812.5 kilometres as the crow flies, by the way – less than the distance between Melbourne and Sydney!

DAY 88: FRIDAY, 11 AUGUST
Mulligan River – no waterhole

A hard day during which I was forced by thick, knee-to-waist high vegetation onto a vehicle track. While on this I passed several artesian springs, all within a kilometre of each other. At the end of the day's march I left the track and I am now camped at a beautiful blow-out, an area stripped bare of vegetation by the wind. Nearby here, and near the springs, is a small dune covered with Aboriginal artefacts. I strolled among them, feeling the power of the stones in the evening light. They speak of great age and always remind me of the transient nature of our little lives.

DAY 89: SATURDAY, 12 AUGUST
Cootadoo Waterhole, Mulligan River

I marched through to here early and then did a major sort of gear. Some hard decisions had to be made but I was ruthless. With so much food and equipment now gone, I was able to take off the tail of the cruiser. The tail consisted of two shafts of wood that rose up from the back of the cruiser at a 30 degree angle. This construction increased the carrying capacity of the cart without reducing its manoeuvrability when weaving through tight vegetation. I stashed the discarded tail with the other jettisoned equipment under some nearby rocks, and made my usual treasure map.

There are no ducks here, so tonight it is freshwater mussels and native pear with my rice.

Tomorrow I shall drop in at Carlo Station and hope that someone is home. They aren't expecting me but I'm keen to get some good advice on the route ahead. I may also ask if they have any decent maps covering the area to the east, of which I have none.

I am also hoping to be able to phone home from the station. I've worked out I may be finished in just 27 more days. This is based on 20 kilometres per day for five days to the Donohue Highway, then 30 kilometres per day from there to the finish. That's 670 kilometres in 22 days. Can I *really* complete this walk in 27 days? Who knows? Certainly not me. The real wild card is that I know so little of the country ahead, but as I approached this waterhole I came into more gibber country just like down south so I hope to have easier travel ahead. Also, things should be quicker once I abandon the cruiser. I hope so; as the trip approaches its conclusion I am approaching my limits.

DAY 90: MONDAY, 13 AUGUST
nowhere

Well if I didn't yesterday, today I've reached the milestone of my furthest walk ever! The South Pole walk was about 1500 kilometres, which I clicked over today. Now I have less than 1000 kilometres to go.

I followed the access track up to Carlo Station where I was hoping to be able to phone Brigitte. Carlo is a funny sort of place. Some biggish sheds and a few portable rooms seem to be about the extent of it. Shirley Jukes was home but her husband, Howard, was out. They are an old couple: Shirley told me Howard is 70.

Shirley has an impressive little vegie patch. They have only been there three years but have been on the land farming all their lives. The station is now on the market and they won't be here much longer. Brigitte and I will drop in on the Jukes on the drive home as my depot is just down the road. Brigitte was not home when I called so I left a message telling her my estimated time of arrival in Burketown is 8 September. (That's her birthday!) There is another station, Cravens Peak, just up the track and I am thinking about calling in there tomorrow to try phoning again. Perhaps she is at the snow; she was planning some training for her Virgin Peaks trip in Antarctica.

Carlo is right on the Tropic of Capricorn, so now I'm in the tropics for the first time since Cape York in 1997. I passed the 'mighty' Toko Range today. In fact, I'd just about passed it before I realised it was actually a mountain range!

Walking on the track is relatively uninspiring and I'll leave it as soon as I can. Just now, however, Seraphine is not handling a certain type of prickle that abounds here. Her working dog boots had helped several times in the first few weeks of the walk, then she lost two digging for a rabbit one day. Her feet have become tougher with time and use, but these are the worst prickles we have come across in a long time so the track is the place to be for now.

Shirley loaned me the map 'Glenormiston' so for the east route I'm now only missing 'Urandangi'. Perhaps someone at Cravens Peak Station has a copy.

The cruiser is really starting to feel light. It was a heavy bag I left yesterday and there's no doubt I'm noticing the difference.

DAY 91: TUESDAY, 14 AUGUST
nowhere, end of the dunes of the Arunta

'You've gotta have a dream. If you don't have a dream,
how you gonna have a dream come true?'

I had another social day on the mission today as I dropped in at Cravens Peak. Seraphine and I were greeted by three pigs and met goats and chooks before running into Colleen McDonald. She looked frightened for a moment; I must look a treat. She seemed to relax when she saw Seraphine, though. I was amazed at what Colleen and her husband, Gordon, had made of the place in just 26 years. Gordon was out picking up relatives so I would have to catch him on the track if I wanted a chat. Colleen gave me a tin of tobacco, and just when I wanted it most, as hunger often returns and I know no better appetite suppressant. I also tried to call Brigitte, but once again could only leave a message on the machine.

So, off I went and marched for a few hours off the track. Unfortunately it was too prickly for Seraphine and desperately slow going, so I reluctantly returned to the road. Further along, I bumped into Gordon, a crusty, classic farmer. He was on his way to get the relatives but was amazed by my mission and stopped to ask lots of questions. He was particularly interested in sampling the bush food I had in my tuckerbag.

Tonight I am in a dry dam, the only place other than the track that is not covered in highly combustible, prickly plants. A pack of dingoes turned up at camp as I was lighting the fire. They started circling us, coming closer and closer, and looking more than just curious. It was dusk and there was enough fire-wood for just another hour, and no trees to climb and nowhere to run. I tied Seraphine to the cruiser and made a big racket, including throwing burning sticks at them. They were not going to be put off so easily and I had no choice but to shoot one. When I did, the rest fled. A moment later Gordon returned along the road with the rellies. He was real happy that I had nailed a dingo; there is a $10 bounty on them, so he chucked it in the back of the ute. I look forward to visiting the McDonalds again on our return.

DAY 92: WEDNESDAY, 15 AUGUST
Pituri Creek, Lake Idamea lower lake

Today was long and hard into a headwind. Perhaps yesterday's distance was a little less than it should have been and perhaps I need a day off sometime soon. I got sandalwood fruits this afternoon for the first time ever – yum! I gorged myself on them and then picked a big bag for later.

I am again on the cusp of a new stage of the journey, as tomorrow I reach the Georgina River. The past three weeks have gone well, since my new beginning from Burt Waterhole. I've traversed the Arunta and covered over 500 kilometres without losing a single day. Despite the good progress, as time goes by I feel an increasing weariness through my entire being. A huge distance remains between me and Burketown, including the most rugged terrain of the entire journey, along the O'Shanassy River. Can I do it?

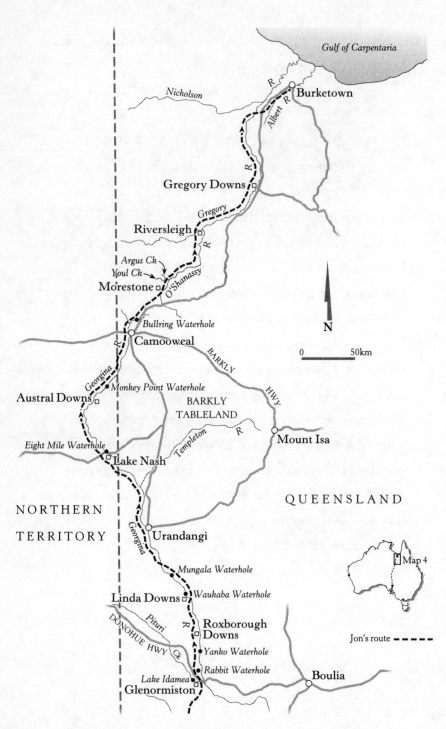

Gulf of Carpentaria

Nicholson

Burketown

Gregory Downs

Gregory

Riversleigh

Argus Ck
Youl Ck
Morestone

O'Shanassy

Bullring Waterhole

Camooweal

BARKLY HWY

Monkey Point Waterhole

Austral Downs

BARKLY
TABLELAND

Eight Mile Waterhole

Templeton R

Mount Isa

Lake Nash

NORTHERN

TERRITORY

QUEENSLAND

Georgina

Urandangi

Mungala Waterhole

Linda Downs

Waukaba Waterhole

Roxborough
Downs

Pituri

DONOHUE HWY

Ck

Yanko Waterhole

Rabbit Waterhole

Lake Idamea

Glenormiston

Boulia

Map 4

Jon's route ▬ ▬ ▬

N

0   50km

MAP 4: GLENORMISTON TO BURKETOWN

8

THE GEORGINA RIVER

Vanishing Horizons

DAY 93: THURSDAY, 16 AUGUST
Rabbit Waterhole, Georgina River

Indecision, then commitment best describes the difficult day I had today. The pressing question was whether I should leave the cruiser at Glenormiston Station or take it on a bit further. In the end I decided to keep it for another four to seven days. We will be more vulnerable without it so I'll keep it as long as I can. Also, I had to consider food. The rations on the cruiser can be strung out for 25 to 30 days depending on what I get along the way.

Last night there were six or so great big pigs in the lake. This was the first time I'd seen wild pigs on the journey, and I was keen to get one. Unfortunately they were all fully grown and it would have been hard to bring one down with my single shot .22 rifle.

This morning I traversed around Lake Idamea lower lake and headed straight for the Georgina River. So far it is better going than I'd expected. I'll be following the Georgina River for well over 400 kilometres so I'm hoping it will be kind to me, with its waterholes full and the environment rich in food. I've never been in any of this country before and know it only through my research.

DAY 94: FRIDAY, 17 AUGUST
Yanko Waterhole, Georgina River

I had a good walk until the last 4 kilometres or so.

This is a much nicer waterhole than the last few ones. There is a yard nearby that is obviously no longer used. I've stopped earlier than usual to try and get some meat, which I haven't had for a few days now. Somehow I seem to have less and less time to get things done though the days are actually getting longer. The sun is now setting at 5.55 p.m. There are many sandalwood trees here with heaps of fruit, but unfortunately it is all still green. Still, something will enjoy it.

If the owners are obliging, I am thinking of leaving the cruiser at Roxborough Downs, a station 16 kilometres north of here. Then I will begin in some ways the most exciting phase of the walk, the lightweight final push. I did the calculations again today in case I speak with Brigitte tomorrow. It is still a long way to go and the words of Dwight Eisenhower keep running through my mind: 'we could still lose this war'. He said this during World War II, when the Germans, who were thought to be all but finished, launched a major offensive against the western allies in the winter of 1944. They initially met with great success, punching a hole through the allies' lines in what became known as the Battle of the Bulge. Sometimes when you are close to success, you are at your most vulnerable.

I tried some fishing but despite getting bites in the waterhole there were no takers. I just keep trying to do everything right; safely and securely. Nonetheless, it's not without some trepidation that I face the dash to the gulf. Uh, 'dash'? Let's hope so, I am starting to feel that it could be more like a crawl to the gulf . . .

DAY 95: SATURDAY, 18 AUGUST
Roxborough Downs Access Track, Georgina River

I did a final morning with the cruiser and then met Haley Sutton at Roxborough Downs. It is a big station with lots of quarters for the 'boys', whom I met briefly, and it even has its own solar-powered public phone. Anyway, Haley had a friend over and there were children and puppies everywhere. Haley didn't look comfortable and I wondered why. After the mission was over, I learned that a couple of British backpackers had been attacked in the Northern Territory and one of them was murdered. The aggressor, who fitted my description, was still on the loose. When I left, Haley called the police who drove several hundred kilometres to look for me but because I walked along the river, away from vehicle roads and tracks, the chance of them spotting me was close to nil.

Haley did not have the 'Urandangi' map or any tobacco, but she had no problems with me leaving the cruiser at the station. I parked it in a shed and attached my gun and stuff sacks to the hauling harness, which now becomes my pack. I left it in the shed to go and call Brigitte from the public phone.

No luck. I left a message and went back to sorting out stuff. I called back at lunchtime, this time with success! So finally, after three goes on three separate days I spoke with my love. We had a decent talk and got through a few of the nitty gritty details but long before we would have said our goodbyes, the solar-powered phone died. I rejoiced in the talk we did have but there was so much more to say. I love her so deeply and it will be wonderful to be together once more. She is driving up alone to collect me in Burketown. Ian and Min Darling may fly to Mount Isa to meet us briefly – Ian has been a driving force in the Great Mission doco and I would love to see him and his wife – but it will be nice to drive home with just the two of us.

Seraphine spent the whole time we were at the station playing with the dogs there and when it was time to go she wanted to stay. She feigned sore feet and whined and gave me her cutest, sad look, with her head tilted to one side. I wasn't fooled and it was hard not to laugh. To get her going I had to pick her up and carry her for the first 100 metres.

The pack is desperately heavy and I will have to go slower

The Georgina River

than I thought, at least to begin with. Walking with a pack is very different from hauling as it uses different muscles. In fact, carrying this glorified backpack is so hard that I am leaving some more stuff right here, at my camp site, just 4 kilometres north of the station! It is stuff I was going to leave behind but threw in at the last moment. Now I know I must leave it; this pack is just too gruesome. It currently weighs about 40 kilograms. Gasp.

The river is beautiful.

DAYS 96–98: SATURDAY, 19 AUGUST TO MONDAY, 21 AUGUST
all over again

What a run-around the past three days has been. On Saturday I had a gruelling walk via the river to get to here, about 35 kilometres north of Roxborough Downs. The pack was very uncomfortable. Thank God I got a duck on the way. On arrival I was horrified to see I'd lost my sleeping mat and bag. Obviously I hadn't tied them to the pack well enough – what a blow.

I left most of my stuff here, placing the food out of harm's, and dingoes' way, up a tree. We retraced our steps as best we could till dark. No luck. I lit two fires and we lay between them. The night was very cold and Seraphine crawled inside my jumper to nestle against my tummy. It was a long night with very little sleep, but luckily I had caught three fish, including

165

one big one (30 centimetres long), so at least we had food. The next morning I walked back to my previous camp near Roxborough Downs, only to find my sleeping gear was not there. I must have walked right past it on the way back here. This meant I had to retrace my steps further, all the way to the station, to pick up my light sleeping bag from the depot before returning to the river to camp. I rang Brigitte again from the station and blurted out my problems. She was calming and reassuring, but obviously disappointed that three days after calling her, I was back in the same place. Emotionally it was a very difficult day.

Today I am back to my bulk gear. On the way here, Seraphine stopped and sniffed at something. She had found my sleeping bag and mat! It is good to have my sleeping mat back, but again I have two sleeping bags when I only need one. Hopefully I can leave the spare at Linda Downs tomorrow, but the whole episode was a 70-kilometre, two-day detour I could have done without. It cost me lots of energy and although I did it almost entirely on protein – duck and fish – I am knackered now.

Also, my big toe is infected and I had to lance it.

DAY 99: TUESDAY, 22 AUGUST
Waukaba Waterhole

Today I used a headband, Nepali style, to help with the load. This consists of a loop of material, in my case my cotton scarf, placed across the top of my forehead and tied to both sides of my pack. This places more load on the neck, but overall the weight is directly over the spine. It has definitely made a difference, reducing the strain on my shoulders. Despite this, the going is quite slow and I'm working hard. Many channels feed into the river from the sides and regardless of where I travel near the river, I face a lot of little ups and downs. My pace up the 'hills' is similar to that of a climber at 8000 metres, painfully slow and laborious. Going down the often steep banks is also slow as I must exercise extreme caution not to slip and fall on the loose earth.

The pluses are that the surroundings are often very picturesque, which is good for morale, and that when I am near the river there is a reasonable amount of shade and the air is cooler. I would be loving it more with a nice comfortable daypack, but then the challenge would be missing. All in all, I would not swap my situation with anyone; despite the hardship, this is a magic trip.

I dropped in at Linda Downs to ask if they could spare a map of the area and met Ben Knight, the manager, and a couple of hands, Jackie and Heath. We had a good yarn and I gained some useful tips from them. They also gave me 12 cigarettes and a few bullets. I borrowed a map of Queensland that has a little more detail than my strip map. If some tobacco, a handful of bullets, the loan of a map and the odd bit of advice are my only concessions to outside assistance, then I will be happy with that. In the overall context of the mission it is all very minor. Without question, the main support I have had on the trip so far has been the 105 kilometres I have walked on vehicle tracks.

Linda Downs is a magic spot, with lots of nice shade and fruit trees. I had to keep moving so I left a depot, just one of my sleeping bags, and came here, to Waukaba Waterhole.

I feel I should take it slowly with the Beast, my nickname for the pack, while it is heavy. But the longer I am out here, the more critical my food supply becomes. My rations alone will not be enough. I am confident the hunting will generally be good along this river, which will help a lot in conserving whatever is left of my carbohydrates and chocolate. At Linda Downs I got some useful advice on pigs so I hope to nail a few piglets soon. Provided there are not too many hiccups I believe I might just scrape through.

DAY 100: WEDNESDAY, 23 AUGUST
between Marbles Bend and Walbo Waterhole

'I thought it would be easy thinking inspiring words . . . it is not. Give Seraphine a scratch on the belly for me! Love B'

Well, that's got me all fired up – I got a pig! Not long after starting this morning I came across a herd of pigs. I dropped my pack and tied Seraphine to it before stalking them for 15 minutes and getting to within 20 metres. From there I fired at a half-grown one and wounded it. The others all took off but the wounded one couldn't keep up. I sprinted after it and only *just* caught it. I had left my knife with my gear so I had no option but to use my rifle as a club to finish it off. In doing so I broke the stock. Never mind, the stock is now glued and taped together and looks fine, and I've got pork. Eight to ten kilograms, in fact, which brings the weight of my pack close to 50 kilograms – itself a total pig!

I thought often about tactics as I staggered through lots of ups and downs over side channels. I now think I will take it *really* slowly up to the top of the river on the Barkly Tableland, then drop a lot of my gear, including boxes, the camera, first aid bits, the solar panel, extra videotapes, the leatherman, the kitbag, the Fairydown bag, the journal, and other odds and ends. I want to try to do the last 275 to 300 kilometres a bit quicker, and I know I'll burn out or injure myself if I push too hard with the weight I'm carrying now. I just hope there will be enough left in the tank to speed up at the end, because if there isn't . . .

DAY 101: THURSDAY, 24 AUGUST
Mungala Waterhole

Another slow and difficult day has forced the hard decision to leave another depot: shot film and video, tripod, camera box. It is only 1.5 to 2 kilograms, but I must lighten the load wherever possible or face defeat. The weight really is killing me, and I feel I would manage so much better with just 5 kilograms less. I shall continue to look over all my gear and see what else I can get rid of. In a week or so it should be easier.

Five and a half hours was all I could manage today but things are going a little better. Today is my 30th consecutive day on the move. Rest day? Maybe a bit further north. These days of longer daylight are allowing me lots of recovery time, though it will be nice to sleep in one day.

DAY 102: FRIDAY, 25 AUGUST
Georgina River

The river is losing its charm. Here there are just small, dirty, isolated puddles, with not a permanent waterhole in sight. Oh well, at least there *is* water, and though the river isn't as pretty, it does generally make for easier going. Things went much better today and the Beast was noticeably lighter.

I saw three plains turkeys on the march today. They are big birds. They got me thinking about the orchard at Hope, where one day there will be a chook empire. It will be large enough to provide us with one or possibly two chooks per week. For the umpteenth time on the trip I wondered about the design of the chookhouse. Should I build it from timber cut from the block and tin from the tip? I reckon. But then, perhaps I could make it out of strawbales!

At the end of the day I am always exhausted. It feels a lot like being at high altitude; a massive effort of will is required to get things done when all one really wants to do is laze about and do nothing. One needs discipline and a sharp focus to stay on top of everything. Now I am rested, though, and everything is done: food, water, fire, etc.

Today I thought of the drive home a lot. I just love a road trip, and the longer the better! It will be wonderful to share it with just my love. The early plan was for someone else to help Brigitte with the drive up but she has decided to do it on her own. She wants me all to herself for the drive home, which is fine by me! It will be a luxurious crossing of the continent, with lots of goodies. Each time I have spoken to her on the phone, I have asked her to bring more of this or that – all my favourite delectable goodies, and all junk food with lots of sugar and fat. No rice, flour or muesli, thank you very much!

The light has been slightly odd today. It is evening just now and a high 'dirty' cloud made for a red setting sun. It makes me think that there must be a big fire north-west some-where. If it turns out to be a rain cloud though, I'll get wet as the tarp is way down south.

I can't help but feel that I am beginning the best part of the trip: the hardest bit. The bit that takes you well beyond your-self and forces you to look long, hard and deep into your soul to find a new understanding of self.

DAY 103: SATURDAY, 26 AUGUST
Georgina River, just north of Urandangi

I picked a decent quantity of Ulcardo melons today, a big bag-ful that will last me many days. I pushed a bit hard, however, and now I'm shattered.

DAY 104: SUNDAY, 27 AUGUST
Georgina River, somewhere

I was feeling strong today with a tailwind to match. Too much of a tailwind perhaps and I went too fast and too far. I should have husbanded my strength better. Now I feel broken.

DAY 105: MONDAY, 28 AUGUST
Georgina River

I have had a slightly shorter day today and I'm not so tired, but there is catching up to do on all fronts: new maps to fold, socks to wash, bread to bake, feet to attend to and so on.

In many places now the river is just one long gutter with several main channels. There are many puddles along it, but on this section there seem to be no permanent waterholes. According to the map, over the border in the Northern Territory there are some good long ones. They start about 35 to 40 kilometres from here, and I hope to have a few days off along that section, to fish, hunt, gather, sort and relax. I'll need to have a very close look at my rations but I think they should see me through provided I get plenty of bush tucker. Speaking of which, I found a full can of beer in the riverbed today! Fair game, I reckon. I've just drunk it and, well, it tasted like warm beer!

My boots were wearing out badly at the heel, which was a worry. But a few days ago I found a shredded inner tube from which I cut sections that I then pulled over my boots so they cover the heel. This works well and has stopped the wearing. Phew – I'd been racking my brains trying to figure out the best solution.

The sight of the gun is off again! I have missed one pig and two ducks over the past few days that I should have got. I will fix it in the morning as I'm desperate for meat.

We had a very cold night last night and for the first time in many weeks there was a dew in the morning. Today I passed the Templeton River, which marks three quarters of the way to Burketown. I must be getting there, then. But I tell you, Australia is a bloody big country to walk across.

DAY 106: TUESDAY, 29 AUGUST
Georgina River in the Northern Territory

At least, I think that's where I am. I've been marching for the past 110 kilometres with nothing but my map of Australia to refer to, which, as you can imagine, doesn't give me much detail! I have simply followed the river, which is relatively unchanging along this section, and though there are many small waterholes, I haven't seen any permanent ones since Mungala, many kilometres back. Of course, I could have missed one as there often seem to be two main channels and several minor ones. Anyway, I am back 'on map' again and there is a good stretch of river that I will reach tomorrow.

My feet are giving me problems and hurt badly for the first 5 to 15 minutes after a break, so I am trying to march longer sessions. I did not expect this. I had hardly a single problem the whole time I was hauling, and now when I switch to carrying, my feet pack it in. It could just be that the orthopaedic pads in my shoes are too worn. I pulled them out just now and they are seriously compressed and thin.

DAY 107: WEDNESDAY, 30 AUGUST
Lake Nash Waterhole, Georgina River

Today was a short day of 15 kilometres. I marched to Lake Nash without stopping, on account of the state of my feet. I did drop in briefly at Lake Nash Station where a woman took my picture for a piece in the local newsletter. They're really nice, these Lake Nash people. Unfortunately I did not meet the boss.

I haven't seen a pig recently but have eaten a swag of freshwater mussels and my big concern now is my feet. I think the problem is that these boots were brand-new at the start of the trip. All I've ever done in them is haul the cruiser and the inside has moulded to accommodate that action. Now that I walk in a more upright position, they are all out of shape. I hope they will give a bit over these next four to five days, otherwise they could stop me. Already my big toe is infected just in behind the nail, though I think this is on the mend. Then there is the hard spot on the outside of my little toe. This has troubled me in the past and is now back with a vengeance.

I have decided to take it easy for the next little while as I'll be camped at good waterholes. At present, it is hard to imagine how I could possibly march 25 kilometres per day as the crow flies and yet a few days back I did it for three days straight. My feet have to improve!

I am very much looking forward to seeing Brigitte again, yet still enjoying the struggle: the best of both worlds.

'Pan Galactic Gargle Blaster from the Natimuk Hotel
Crème de cacao, dark
Full cream, lots
Orange juice, a good squeeze
Tequila, enough
Sun setting, holding wife's hand
Waves crashing'

DAY 108: THURSDAY, 31 AUGUST
unnamed waterhole, Georgina River

I moved on today. I had really planned to take a day off but without making a conscious decision, I packed up and continued. Perhaps rather than taking a few entire days off, I'll march a few short days, resting in the afternoons. My feet are a bit better today, mostly because I only walked half a day yesterday so I've done the same today.

Immediately on arrival at this waterhole I shot a big fat duck. Seraphine jumped in the water, swam out and brought it in. Five minutes later I added a pig to my larder! It was medium-sized and shot at very close range. I spent the afternoon dealing with it and getting lots of fat from it, which I usually make into 'fat cakes'. These are large slabs of fat that I place on the bottom, inside walls and underside of the lid of my alloy billy-cum-camp-oven. To hold the fat in place I pack the centre with meat. When cooked on the fire the result is delicious crackling lined with fat. All up it should last me a while. I also roasted a hind leg. I have more meat than I can possibly eat. Yahoo!

The country is more undulating away from the river, but is generally good going. I am really so immersed in this journey that it is hard to imagine it will, or even can, come to an end. I am really not counting the days despite the new 'days remaining' column in the log. That is there so I can give Brigitte a clear idea of when I may finish. An exact finish date is too hard to predict, though, with so many variables in the equation.

The feast I obtained here will last me several days and I think I should have a good run over the next four days or so. I'll take it easy, rest my feet and feed up a bit before facing the crossing of the Barkly Tableland.

Seraphine had me in stitches of laughter earlier today, when she disappeared into the long, dry grass bordering the river. She was excitedly following a scent and every now and again she would spring straight up, and appear above the grass for a moment to peer around, before falling back down.

I am looking at another incredible red sunset, like the one I experienced four or five days ago. It has been an odd day weather-wise, with very strong headwinds, an odd assortment of clouds, and a strange dirty light all day. Now the sun is really red, the very strong wind of the day has gone and a big dark cloudbank is rolling in from the west. Will it rain? I have prepared for it as best I can but the bottom line is, if it rains a lot, I get wet! It isn't a problem to keep it out of the essentials. It's just me and my sleeping bag that will get wet. Seraphine sleeps in my bag so she'll be all right! I am camped under low branches so if it is just a light shower I'll be fine.

DAY 109: FRIDAY, 1 SEPTEMBER
Eight Mile Waterhole, Georgina River

Happy anniversary, darling! Let's go to the beach and celebrate our 18th wedding anniversary. Let's eat and drink well, go for a few nice strolls, go beachcombing, and sit on the dune crest with the setting sun. All in good time.

As for the here and now, I had a good day marching along the river, past many permanent waterholes. My feet are a bit better, but it was time to stop when I did.

DAY 110: SATURDAY, 2 SEPTEMBER

I haven't camped yet. I felt weak on the march this morning and I have decided to take a long break here at Junction Water-hole. I'm planning to get out and do a bit more this evening.

Georgina River

I did better on my evening march. That long afternoon siesta did the trick.

DAY 111: SUNDAY, 3 SEPTEMBER
Monkey Point Waterhole, Georgina River

I spoke with Brigitte today!

I had my earliest start yet, this morning, with the help of the moon. The batteries in my head torch are now well into the 48–150 hour zone and the torchlight is dim. In the early morning

I dropped in at Austral Downs Station and spoke with the manager, Dave Roberts, who was friendly and helpful. He used to work on Morstone, a station to the north that I will shortly walk across, and gave me advice about it, including not to follow my plan of descending the O'Shanassy River. Dave described the country down there as extremely rocky and rugged. He said I'd be lucky to do 5 kilometres in a day. Hmm, food for thought.

I rang Brigitte from the station and had a good talk. I was keen to hear her news and although I didn't want to hog the line for too long, we had a decent chat. It is hard to believe that in a little over two weeks the mission should be completed. I am now into my fifth calendar month out here!

The plains in this part of the country are amazing and in many places there is not a tree in sight, except along the river, of course. When I'm marching on these plains, I experience a sensation I'm familiar with from my time in Antarctica – the featureless horizon simply keeps receding as you walk, giving you the feeling that you are walking on a treadmill and going nowhere.

This journey is taxing like no other I have been on. I can feel my energy, my body, myself slowly being drained. It is amazing, though, the difference a big feed of meat makes. Yesterday evening I got another small duck, which I will have with a bit of rice this evening. My meat doesn't keep for more than two to two-and-a-half days here, compared to up to eight days down south. Speaking with Brigitte also always has a good effect on my energy. Along with the meat over the past few days, it has helped slow the drain.

It is getting hotter all the time. Spring has arrived and I was supposed to have finished by now, according to my original plan. Heat is something I've never handled so well – I sweat more and so need to drink more. When I have to work hard, I'm better in the cold. It is often still quite cold at night but I wonder if it is just that my seriously depleted body notices it more. At present my confidence is good but a spell without meat will leave me wondering. As always on the mission there are plenty of greens, but these alone don't satisfy me.

DAY 112: MONDAY, 4 SEPTEMBER
a wander in the night

What an epic today turned out to be! It started well when I got a duck first thing in the morning. Then the wind dropped and it became very hot. At that point the river was a series of minor channels 3 kilometres across with no good animal tracks, or at least none that I could find, so we were pushing through long grass. Seraphine was working hard and became heat-stressed so we stopped. I went in search of water but found none and we didn't have a lot left in reserve. At 5 p.m. we marched 15 kilometres due north away from the river to a bore. It was dry! So we trekked due east back to the river, where we found water at 2 a.m. We had marched 42 kilometres in 16 hours. Sometime during the march we crossed the border and are now back in Queensland.

DAY 113: TUESDAY, 5 SEPTEMBER
a puddle, 10 km south of the Barkly Highway

We had a short march today as we were both worn out. We will cross the Barkly Highway tomorrow. Seven pigs turned up to drink from the puddle that I'm camped by and settled just 8 or 9 metres away, so I shot one. Yahoo!

My feet are still painful but are not crippling me. Overall they are on the mend but I'm concerned they will blow up again when I begin to descend from the tableland to the lowlands of the Gulf of Carpentaria. By all accounts it is very rough country.

I have been holding back on my stores for a while in case we are faced with unforeseen delays. I am very short on flour, with only enough for two tiny loaves each the size of a fist, and with more than 300 kilometres left to walk . . .

DAY 114: WEDNESDAY, 6 SEPTEMBER
Bullring Waterhole, Chester Creek, Barkly Tableland

I am now on a tributary of the Georgina River and approaching the 'summit' of the Barkly Tableland. Tomorrow or the day after I'll begin descending towards the sea. The terrain is changing yet again, with different trees, termite mounds, and some different grasses. This waterhole is a nice one. There is a pile of rocks forming a small cliff and on top of it is a rock figtree. It is absolutely loaded but the fruit is unripe bar a few dozen, which are delicious. I shot a duck on arrival. Both Seraphine and I are a bit tired but we have much more energy than usual after all the pork we have been eating. This kill should last till tomorrow night.

DAY 115: THURSDAY, 7 SEPTEMBER
near B. Bore

'I look forward to seeing you again, and to listening to your stories of wild days out there.'

That's probably about 12 days away now, because I am over! Over the crest of the Barkly Tableland, the watershed between the Lake Eyre basin to the south and the Gulf of Carpentaria to the north. For well over 1000 kilometres, in fact since I left Lake Eyre, I have been ever so slowly climbing to 250 metres above sea level. Now I have begun my descent to the sea. Burketown is just 265 kilometres away, less than the distance from Melbourne to Hope. This now feels like the home stretch. The actual 'home run' will hopefully begin once I am down off the tableland.

It was weird out there on the 'Pampas'. The going was relatively good on animal tracks that wove their way through the mid-thigh to chest high grass. But they constantly petered out and then it was slow till we picked up the next. The grass is very thick and long in places and I had to carry Seraphine several times over 100 to 500 metre stretches of it. Tomorrow morning I'll join the track to Morstone. It is not far from here and I would have to go a long way off route to avoid the station road. It is the only logical route.

There is a tiny hut here made up of two wee tin rooms, one with a chimney, slowly decaying; I am on the verandah.

The days are just flying by. It is incredible how quickly time can pass. At present my well-fed body feels stronger than it has for many days but by tomorrow lunchtime the duck will be gone and unless I have a successful hunt between now and then, the hunger and terrible weakness will return.

DAY 116: FRIDAY, 8 SEPTEMBER
the junction of Youl and Argus creeks

We were away early, marching the 14 kilometres down the track to the station. It was a full moon and I took advantage of it, minimising the hours I would have had to march in the heat of the day. Also, today I really wanted to speak with someone who knows the country, and the earlier I arrived at Morstone, the more likely it was that somebody would be home.

Before the first glimmer of daylight I saw headlights. As soon as I am on a vehicle track, even just a station track, there is a car! Even at 4.30 a.m. It was the boys from Morstone, going out to some yards to draft the cattle. They were amazed to see me and told me that the boss would be along shortly in a truck. They called him on the radio to tell him: 'There's a guy out here walking who wants to talk to you.' The lads couldn't answer my questions as they hadn't been down to the O'Shanassy, where I am headed. So Graeme Dale turned up and stopped. He was off to work and didn't have much time to spare but the route sounds good so far as water is concerned. I told him I was crossing the continent, headed for Burketown.

'You're going the wrong way! Go back to the main road and head down that.'

'I want to go down the O'Shanassy.'

'You'll get lost!'

'I'm experienced.'

Once that was established he was very helpful with advice. I then stopped at the station where I met Robin and the kids.

Morstone is a nice place with lots of vegies and trees. I rang home and got the answering machine, but then Brigitte cut in! We had a good talk and I wished her a happy birthday. There is a tremendous excitement now that the mission, soon to enter its fifth month, is almost over and we shall be together once more. We couldn't hog the line too long though, and discussion over the details of the meeting and what's happening with the business always takes a while, so we kept it practical.

Robin and I had a long chat and the kids were very interested. They said I looked funny. Robin asked if I wanted to look in the mirror. No thanks! She gave me more details on the nature of the river and things in general, having lived here for nine years herself. I am expecting the next 70 kilometres to be the most rugged part of the traverse, so I am looking forward to that. I do feel like I'm just flying through the landscape but I try to have a good long look at it all as I go.

I have been underguesstimating the temperatures in my log. Yesterday it was 33°C in Mount Isa, and I guesstimated it at 26°C – way out. I think this is a subconcious ploy of mine to try to make it seem cooler than it really is.

Today I was blessed with a feed of big, fat, juicy mistletoe.

There has been a surreal light up here these past few days. The wind-blown dust is creating a dirty haze that is very obvious around the flat, unbroken, golden horizon.

Life outside the mission is a little more on my mind as the trip draws to a close. I have all sorts of work to do: guided trips to organise and lead, slide shows to give, and a lot of mowing, slashing and clearing of fallen branches. Although my home life is getting closer, and my thoughts turn there a little more regularly than earlier in the trip, it does increasingly feel like someone else's life I'm thinking about. A long expedition is a life unto itself; it contains joys and sorrows, conquests and setbacks, highs and lows, and for its duration there is no other.

9

THE O'SHANASSY RIVER

Lost to the World

DAY 117: SATURDAY, 9 SEPTEMBER
5 km downstream from Old Morestone

It has been a terrible day – Seraphine is dead. She must have eaten a poison dingo bait. Not long after we arrived at the ruins of Old Morestone Station she was sick, then she started acting very strangely – yelping, tucking her tail between her legs, hiding in corners, being sick again, foaming at the mouth, fitting, convulsing, dead – all in the space of 10 minutes. I am totally devastated and can't motivate myself to keep going just now. I have buried her here with her remaining dry food. It is a heavy burden to bear alone. Was I wrong to bring her on the mission? Just like me, she lived 10 000 lives out here on the long march, and I guess I can be thankful for that. I always knew it was a risk to bring her, but life is risky – would she have been safer at home? I was feeling broken and weary before this, but now the emotional drain on top of my already weakened state could just swing the balance in the wrong direction. It is going to be very hard to walk away from here.

I eventually left, with tears streaming down my cheeks into my beard. A large part of me now sees the trip, regardless of the outcome, as a failure. I have failed Seraphine: I failed my own rule of taking good care of my partner/team and I failed my promise to Brigitte to look after Seraphine. It has been a nightmarish day.

'It's a terrible thing to lose a companion in this way,' wrote Robert Falcon Scott on the return march from the South Pole in 1912, after the death of Petty Officer Evans. Indeed, it was terrible. I held Seraphine in her last minutes, and felt her tiny heart beat its last. People will no doubt ask what was the hardest part of the trip and surely it can't get any grimmer than that. The only thing for me to do now is push even harder. This will distract me from upsetting thoughts, and help me get to sleep more easily.

DAY 118: SUNDAY, 10 SEPTEMBER
O'Shanassy River

It feels like a different world down here. It's a very beautiful place and is soothing for an emotionally unstable Jon. There are palms and many great trees on the banks and in the river.

The escarpment is made of beautiful grey limestone that forms cliffs up to 20 metres high. Mostly it is all broken down into giant piles of rock. There are lots of freshwater crocodiles and I saw six dive in the water along a 1-kilometre stretch of a very deep, long, unbroken pool. It would be a beautiful place to live.

The river is all spring water. The top section, at Old Morestone, just peters out into the sand, after which there is a 20-kilometre dry stretch with just one semipermanent waterhole, Pelican Waterhole. The dry bed proved a fast route, though there were some long stretches of very heavy sand. Once I hit the next set of springs, I moved back up onto the animal pads along the banks. These are mostly good going but have many fallen trees that I must climb over, and branches and tall shrubs that I have to duck under. The bending down is difficult as the gun's barrel sits somewhat higher than my head and back.

Mentally I have put yesterday's trauma largely behind me. I have had to distract myself at times, though, as my thoughts often stray there. I must now begin to look to the future, but not too far. I think from here the water should be mostly continuous to the gulf.

Relax. I must try and relax my mind from its present torment – from hunger and from Seraphine – as best as possible, and use the energy in a more positive fashion. Like getting this wreck of a body to tidal salt water. I made my last bread today and put a load of figs in it but it is still pitifully small.

DAY 119: MONDAY, 11 SEPTEMBER
O'Shanassy River

It was a beautiful but very gruelling day along the river. There are animal pads everywhere and loads of pigs. (I got a piglet.) I also saw lots of beautiful pale grey wallabies and freshwater crocodiles, including several small ones a foot long. Along the river there are lovely orange streaked walls of limestone, 50 to 60 metres high, with dark deep caves in places. The twelve-year-old in me desperately wants to climb up the short slope to explore them. Some have distinctive blackened streaks on their ceilings, evidence of the fires of Australia's first people, who used the caves over many thousands of years. I stopped by one of the long, deep pools for a break and threw in a line and caught a fish. It was hot and I sweated buckets.

The terrain was mostly very difficult today and because of my tired condition, I'm stumbling a little more than I normally would in such country. Either trails petered out or I had to push through low undergrowth pulling many branches out of the way. Around here the going is all ups and downs in swampy channels leading off the main one. A number of times I found myself on peninsulas, having to backtrack up to 500 metres to get around them. Then just before I stopped, the nature of the river changed. The low rocky hills and cliffs that previously came right in to the banks of the river are now separated from it by a level, relatively open 'plain' that allows for fairly fast going. I am hoping for a continuation of the better travelling conditions tomorrow.

There are plenty of figs along these river banks, of all different types: cluster, sandpaper and rock. Fortunately there is ripe fruit on all of them.

My pack, my boots and my pants are all slowly falling apart and there is a hunger it seems no amount of meat, fruit and greens can cure. But my feet continue to slowly improve and I have no aches and pains, just an increasing heavy weariness. Indeed there is a protest emanating from the very core of my soul. The endless march, the heat, the mosquitoes, the prickles; my will issues strict orders to press on regardless. My conscious mind does not have the strength to argue. I believe I have the reserves to complete the mission, but as always I must be careful and play my cards right.

There is a herd of brumbies living around here. As I was making dinner the stallion pranced up and down about 25 metres away while the other nine looked on, snorting and neighing.

It is currently an hour and a half after dark and it is hot. I'm lying on my mat with sweat pouring off me. Maybe it is because I have just eaten a piglet! The mozzies are attacking me as usual and I found half a dozen tiny ticks on me today. I think they lived on the pigs and jumped ship when I strapped the pigs on my pack.

So, another day has absolutely flown by. It is non-stop and although I am now quite close to the end, it is not something I dwell on. There is too much here to absorb me. Always on the march my mind wanders to those who once lived everywhere I have walked. I see evidence of their culture, and feel the presence of their spirit.

DAY 120: TUESDAY, 12 SEPTEMBER
O'Shanassy River

One hundred and twenty incredible days! I had always guesstimated that the Great Mission would take between 90 and 120 days. I guessed wrong!

It has been another amazing, hot day along the river with a number of beautiful cliffs to enjoy. I can't stop marvelling at the magnificent trees in the river valley. I got another piglet and nine fish this evening, and gathered figs and some water lilies as well, but it all takes time.

Studying the last bit of the route, from here to Burketown, I can't see how I can finish on the 19th. That would mean averaging 28.5 kilometres per day. *Australian Geographic* is trying to organise coverage of my arrival, so they need a fixed date. But this is easier said than done. I don't have enough dry food left to get me to Burketown, so I must go even slower, stretching the little I have further but allowing me time to hunt and gather. This is the only way I can make it.

Tomorrow I will be passing through Riversleigh Station and I will speak with either Brigitte or Ian Darling at Mission Control. It will be hard to break the terrible news of Seraphine's death and this is something I've been dreading, but it must be done. I want Brigitte to have a few days to come to terms with it before our reunion.

The O'Shanassy is good water. It is the first time in over 2000 kilometres I can actually see through my water. Most of it has been cloudy at best, but really, all the water on the march has been good and I have not been sick once though I have treated none of it.

I am marching without stopping these days as beginning again after short rests is too painful on my feet and body. Each time I start marching, the stiffness, aches and blisters take a long time to settle down to a point where the pain is bearable. If I stay still for more than a minute or so, I must go through the whole excruciating process again. I only stop for gathering and hunting, which means that the only time I get to relax now is when everything is done and all is organised for a quick get-away in the morning.

I was lucky to find some ripe sandpaper figs today. There are heaps of sandpaper figtrees about but most have no fruit at all, and the few that do are loaded with unripe figs. How can I possibly make the 200 kilometres to Burketown on just three food bars, two chocolate bars, less than 900 grams of rice, 650 grams of muesli, 50 grams of Ensure (a nutritious alternative to milk powder) and a lump of bread that doesn't even cover the palm of my hand? If I was fresh and hadn't just done 120 days, no problem. But now, not a chance. The hunting and gathering had better be good.

Tomorrow I reach the twelfth and final stage of the mission, the Gregory River. Fingers crossed that we will get on well!

10

THE GREGORY RIVER

At My Limit

DAY 121: WEDNESDAY, 13 SEPTEMBER
Gregory River

It was the usual story today: a long and difficult day during which I covered a lot of ground but didn't progress far. When I struggle up the short steep rises out of the ravines I feel like I am above 8000 metres high. Every step requires a huge effort of will and even though I'm not suffering from oxygen starvation, I move at the pace of a one-hundred year old.

The Gregory River is beautiful. It's fast in places, over rocky bits of a sort of slate, but never for long, and big, slow-flowing pools break it up. On both sides of the river are small, rounded rock hills with occasional short cliff lines. The river up here is very similar to the O'Shanassy but with more water and much wider. I imagine that when it leaves the mountains behind and begins its final journey across the flat gulf savannah to the sea it will be very different. There was once a vehicle track down here, but often I can't find any trace of it so I've been following the animal pads, as usual. A freshwater crocodile is lying on the other side of the pool by which I am camped. It is perched on the top of a partially submerged branch that is smaller than it is, making the crocodile look like it's sitting on top of the water.

Three times today I had to ford rivers. This slows me down a lot as each time I must stop, first to remove my boots, then again to dry my feet, etc. I headed down the west bank of the river and came across a long deep channel full of water that I had to traverse around. That little exercise took me on a 2-kilometre detour to gain just 100 metres in the right direction. I can't complain, though, it was a nice detour.

Finally I arrived at Riversleigh Station; I had been further from it than I thought. Riversleigh is owned by the local Aboriginal people but no one was there, so I left a note to ask if they could call Mission Control with messages. Shortly after, down at the river, a station ute pulled up. It was Keith Chapman, the station manager.

Keith said he had spoken with Kate, Ian's secretary, and left my messages. I asked him about crocs and water, then out came the map and we discussed my proposed route. Keith asked if I had a radio, which of course I don't, and then proceeded to tell me about the hijacked planes and the World Trade Centre. It is the only piece of 'news' I have received on the trip, and it comes from another world. A world so bizarre, so violent, so out of place on this beautiful planet. When

Homo sapiens' time is up on earth, I imagine all surviving species will breathe a sigh of relief and think, 'Weren't they a pack of animals.'

To Hope it must be then, where I can be surrounded by nature. Well, not quite like on this trip, but I can't stay out here forever. At the end of the day I am, like all of us, a social animal. Though the need is great and the urge irresistible to get away and be alone, I shall always return to those that I love and, therefore, the world of people.

Today I found more figs, water lilies and bulrush and a few dozen old, dried conkerberries. These are a small, red fruit and are very sweet, just what I wanted. Mostly I ate what I found on the spot, though I brought a swag of rush and fig to add to dinner and brekkie respectively.

I have never been so hungry for so long. On climbing expeditions you are never long gone from the fleshpots of Base Camp. The South Pole walk was the closest I have come to this constant feeling of hunger, though then it only lasted for several weeks. I'll be taking tobacco and a few more treats when we head to the North Pole; down south this was sorely missed.

So finally I have less than 200 kilometres to go. For some reason, more than 200 kilometres starts to sound like a lot and less than 200 kilometres is a short walk. Here I am at the beginning of Stage 12 and all I have to do is a short walk down the Gregory! I am feeling very worn-out and the needle says it is empty, but there still seems to be something in the tank. How long can I keep going like this? Never before have I pushed so hard for so long, and I feel closer to the limits of my endurance than ever before. It is a great place to be.

DAY 122: THURSDAY, 14 SEPTEMBER
Gregory River bank, near point 175 m

I like this country and the river has been kind; good animal pads a kilometre or so from the river make for pretty fast going and although I still have dry watercourses to cross, out further they are less frequent.

My route-finding took me a bit too far west and at the end of the day I found myself separated from the river by a range of rocky hills. These small hills are beautiful, with many different rock types about and cliffs of all colour, form and size. I enjoyed being amongst them as I crossed over to regain the river after the day's march.

I passed thousands of conkerberries today and 'snacked out' on them, regularly stopping for a minute to eat a dozen or so. Sweet and delicious. I also have more fresh meat today: a very tender young pig.

The watercourses feeding into the river are veritable miniature canyons, with very steep, sometimes vertical, walls of earth up to 15 metres high. They often branch off and have mostly flat, sandy bottoms. The wind blows fiercely in places like this and I must be particularly careful: an injury now would be a difficult pill to swallow.

The mission, the mission, the mission. I must keep up my guard till the end. These are very hard days. My mind wanders back to yesterday's comments about my need to be a social animal. Despite the truth of those feelings, I am not especially looking forward to returning to that bizarre world of madness out there.

DAY 123: FRIDAY, 15 SEPTEMBER
Gregory River somewhere

Day 123 was another long and oh-so-difficult day. My pack feels like it is not getting lighter anymore. Also I get light-headed if I stand up too quickly and sometimes when the going is rough I stagger about like a drunk. I still have 141 kilometres to go as the crow flies. I fell asleep during one afternoon break and I know the next several days will push me even further. I have been moving non-stop for 53 days. That's a new record for me, beating my 50 days in Antarctica. I feel I can make it but only just. My entire being screams out STOP. A small pig for dinner has revived my energy a little, but I need bulk carbohydrates and sugar.

Today marks the end of four months on the mission. It's just amazing that I have been able to stay in the field unsupported and on the move for so long. This has been the most incredible journey I have been on and in many ways it will not be easy to let it go. Letting the 11-year dream, that has now become reality, fade to memory will be the difficult thing. This is always much harder on a solo trip because there will never be anybody to get together with to reminisce and relive past glories, epics, disasters and laughs. Nevertheless, I've gained more than simply memories. The experiences I've had and lessons I've learned will remain with me and provide strength and a great clarity of vision and understanding of the nature of Australia, the earth, and myself. I will hold this for the rest of my days.

DAY 124: SATURDAY, 16 SEPTEMBER
Gregory River, 10 km north of Gregory Downs

I dropped in at Gregory Downs Station and got some advice on the route ahead. I also called Mission Control on the public phone in front of the pub. Cars were driving past and a few dogs lay in the dust, and on the other side of the country Ian picked up the phone. I could picture in my mind the view from his office window of Sydney Harbour Bridge and the hustle and bustle of a big city. Ian will pass on a message to Brigitte, who has started on her drive to Burketown to pick me up. It was good to have a yarn with a friend, especially one as close to the mission as he is. Ian said things looked promising as far as the film goes, and he was impressed with the shots up to Kalamurra, which Brigitte took home after meeting me on the Warburton.

I got a swag of figs today, though I had to climb a tree to get most of them, and another small pig for dinner. Unfortunately I had to carry it for most of the day as I shot it very early, but I must take the opportunities as they present themselves.

Now I am really closing in on the gulf. It is incredible to see such a big body of water on my next map. Am I really going to do it this time? Or will I stumble somehow in the next four days or so, and blow it? The outside world holds little appeal just now. The struggle consumes me completely, and I am finding it all so rewarding.

DAY 125: SUNDAY, 17 SEPTEMBER
Gregory River

Today was very long and hard, with no pig at the end of it! I am leaving some stuff at this camp site to lighten my load for the last four days. The camera ran out of battery, giving me the perfect excuse to finally ditch that instrument of torture. It has been great to talk to, but it is just too heavy. I am leaving my gun too; hopefully I'll get enough food from the river to get me to Burketown. In fact, today I caught a small fish. I also picked yet more figs.

Weary to the bone.

DAY 126: MONDAY, 18 SEPTEMBER
Gregory River

I'm actually feeling a little stronger today as I have eaten much better. Over the past four or five weeks I have been eating less than my already meagre ration to guard against unforeseen delays. Now, with only two days to go, I can tuck in a bit more. At the end of a meal I am still not totally satisfied, but with no gun and no fish this evening, I am thankful for the little extra rice and muesli.

The plan for tomorrow is that Brigitte will meet up with me about 24 kilometres from Burketown. Whoever gets to the Camooweal road sign first will leave a message with directions to the other's camp site. It is incredible to be in this position. I have been so focused all the time that the end really has crept up on me!

Animal tracks come and go along the river here and I have been following them on and off. From here, though, the only logical way to go is to head away from the river and march to the meeting point. I will march tonight to arrive first thing in the morning and in so doing may actually reach tidal salt water tomorrow! This all depends on how far it is, of course, and I may not reach it till the following day, but for me this is the real objective – arrival at tidal salt water will mark the end of the crossing of this continent. Despite that, I shall finish the actual walk at Burketown.

Suddenly I am feeling nervous. What will it be like to be

with people again? There may even be some press there to film, photograph and interview. How could I ever find the right words to describe and to explain the mission? I'll do my best, but words really are too limited.

A lizard has just wandered slowly by, doing a curious dance with its front legs. It stops, lifts one leg, then the other in the air, waves them for 5 or 10 seconds then moves a short distance and does it all again. Wow – some sort of gull has just flown by. I am not sure exactly what kind, but it is definitely a sea bird!

What I have most difficulty with back in the not-so-real world is the often complicated nature of our daily round. Filling in forms, standing in queues, making 'important' calls, and having to conform to a whole social structure that is a very, very long way from that by which we have lived since the dawn of Homo sapiens, has always been a problem for me, but I am sure I will never have felt it so acutely as after this mission.

A team expedition has its own social structure, and because this has been my longest solo trip, things may be a little odd for a while. The trip home, camping en route and slowly re-visiting the few people I've met along the way will help me acclimatise.

I just saw a blue winged kookaburra. It was turquoise really and just beautiful. This riverbank makes a nice camp site. It is cool and green here, and there is good deep shade in many places. There are myriad noises both day and night.

DAY 127: TUESDAY, 19 SEPTEMBER
the crossing of Beames Brook and Albert River

What a big day it has been! I have just walked unsupported across a continent!

I got away at midnight after not being able to sleep and being plagued by mozzies like never before on the trip. I headed down a station track to a more major road and then on to our meeting point. There was no Brigitte, but there was a message from her from yesterday. She was at the caravan park in Burketown and would be back in a few hours, at midday.

I desperately wanted to finish so I headed down the Albert River till I reached the tidal zone, the part of the river where the fresh water coming down the river battles with the tides bringing in the sea.

I had done it. There was no euphoria or wild gesticulating or sounds of conquest. Just the deep satisfaction that I had completed my main objective, the traverse of Australia.

I walked back out to the main road and sat under the meagre shade of a small tree. Brigitte had been driving up and down the road looking for me. I was so tired from the mission, and from no sleep and a big day, that there was no energy for emotional displays. Sitting in the dust by the roadside we hugged, then we found a place to camp. Tomorrow I shall finish the last stretch to Burketown, where a small reception is waiting. Apparently the local schoolkids will welcome me.

The satisfaction of trips like this is gained in small doses along the way, day-by-day, and is not waiting in one parcel at the end. On more than half my expeditions the physical objective has not been reached, but I consider very few of them to have been unsuccessful. Indeed, from *my* perspective, some of my most successful expeditions have been those that have not reached the objective. What is the meaning of success? For me it is to be safe, to enjoy and to learn. It is nice to reach the goal, the cherry on top of the cake, but I have always been more interested in the cake. I can take or leave the cherry, but it's great purpose is to make you strive for it. The peak, the summit, the top, the best, the first all hold little meaning for me. The rock on the mountain top beyond which there are no more rocks is just another rock, holding no more relevance or meaning than the great pyramid of rock below it. Our obsession with 'the best' zeros us all in on that one rock and we lose sight of the pyramid, impoverishing both ourselves and our society. I don't believe this has always been so for Homo sapiens, but rather that it is another symptom of the evolutionary blind alley down which we are running at top speed.

Brigitte has driven the 26 kilometres to town to do a few things, and I am lying under the green tropical canopy that envelopes the creek, staring upwards and thinking nothing in particular. There is a slight vacuum, an emptiness, and a sadness that the great mission is basically over. I will do one last march to Burketown in the morning but the dream that has enriched my life so fully is now realised, and now it is time to move on. A large part of me wants to cling to it and not let go but I must, or, like a sinking ship, it will drag me down. It is now very nearly in the past and I must continue to live in the present and dream of the future.

DAY 128: TUESDAY, 20 SEPTEMBER
Burketown

The journey is over. One final march into a strong headwind and heavy dust and I'm there, or here. Brigitte took lots of film and someone pulled over to ask, 'Are you the bloke headed south–north?'

'No, he's a few hundred metres behind!'

'Congratulations!'

The school kids and a few locals were out to meet me. I went to the water's edge and Brigitte shot some film. The kids asked me a million questions – my first press conference! Then they went back to school.

I walked to the edge of the mudflats and placed half my shell from Port Augusta in the waters. (The other half I have kept as a souvenir of the mission.) I watched it float for a while then sink. It had travelled with me, all the way from the cold Southern Ocean to these warm tropical waters.

From there I limped the 150 metres to the car and we drove to the Burketown caravan park for me to have a shower.

When in a vehicle for the first time after a long journey on foot I always find myself having to suppress an urge to tell the driver to slow down. We travelled less than a kilometre and went no faster than 60 kilometres per hour, but I still felt like we were approaching the speed of light and felt very vulnerable. The human animal is not designed to go faster than running pace! Once at the caravan park, the face that stared at me in the mirror was aged, haunted, the body wasn't mine.

Then there was a seemingly endless round of phone interviews with radio and TV stations and newspapers. The people at the Shire office here have been *fantastic*, and have given us our own phone and desk! Brigitte is coordinating everything, which is just as well as I am incapable to, but I do seem to manage the actual interviews. As usual, most interviewers ask the common, mundane, easy questions, but there are two or three who go deeper than the surface and these force me to use my mind in a way that I haven't for over four months.

Eating, eating, eating. In the 4-hour march this morning, I ate more sugar and chocolate than in the previous two weeks! Brigitte has brought many boxes full of all sorts of food and it was hard to know where to begin. So far I've tucked in to salt and vinegar chips, chocolate, cake, olives, chicken and beer.

The locals are blown away and interested and enthusiastic. The Shire presented me with a beautiful pen and letter opener set made by one of their members from conkerberry timber. I have been overwhelmed by the response.

I saw a segment on the ABC news which used some of my footage from early in the trip and it looks good.

I am very tired, but still sleep eludes me. Just now I can only think of one word . . . Yahoo!

The Great Mission – they said it couldn't be done!

EPILOGUE

In the days and weeks following my arrival at Burketown, my body felt broken like never before. I had lost 23 kilograms in body weight during the mission; there wasn't a gram of fat on me and my muscles were thin and wasted. The lines on my face were very pronounced and I looked 20 years older than I was. I felt twice my age, too, and hobbled around looking like I'd just made the first unsupported traverse of the continent. I'm always amazed how the will – the psyche – can keep a body going further than most people would believe possible. Once the goal is reached and safety assured, the body falls in a heap and it is only then that you realise how far beyond yourself you have gone. Brigitte took care of me and attended to most of the physical tasks that needed doing.

We spent a few days in Burketown, where the locals really looked after us. I was in no rush to move on and there were a few things we wanted and needed to do, such as interviews and the like. Really, after marching the last 57 days straight I just felt like staying in one place for at least a few days.

During our stay, a boat was arranged to take us out through the mangroves to the open waters of the Gulf of Carpentaria. As I looked out over the blue waters of the sea my mind wandered to Burke and Wills, the first to traverse the continent. With no boat they were unable to enjoy this view, but reaching tidal salt water must have given them an over-whelming feeling of satisfaction that their expedition had succeeded in its objective.

On the trip home, Brigitte and I camped for several nights by a beautiful secluded waterhole on the Gregory River, where we found a suitable headstone for Seraphine's grave. Brigitte painted it with the inscription:

Little Miss Puppy
Seraphine Snupesen
9.9.99 – 9.9.2001

The following day we called in to Morstone Station, where we were greeted by Robin. She was saddened to hear of Seraphine's death and gave us her blessing to drive down to Old Morestone.

It was difficult to return to the ghostly ruins, though some-thing we both felt we needed to do. We placed the headstone on the grave and built a small fence around the lot. Once again I left with tears in my eyes.

From Morstone, we slowly drove south across the conti-nent, picking up my various stashes of equipment and rocks, and visiting the station owners I had met on the march. Every-one was happy to see us and wanted to hear how I'd gotten on after I'd passed through. They all commented on how thin and haggard I looked, particularly Malcolm and Colleen Mitchell, who were the first people I'd seen on the walk, when I still looked relatively fresh.

The continent flashed past in a blur of brown earth and red rocks. Travelling this way gives you an overview of what the country looks like, but you don't fully experience it. All the subtlety is lost and being inside a car is like being inside a spaceship: you can see the outside, but not hear, smell, touch or taste it. The distance seemed enormous, even taking relatively straight lines and travelling 70 to 100 kilometres per hour. It went on forever and really brought home to me that indeed I had walked across the continent.

Arriving home after a long absence is always a strange time for me. I experience everything with the heightened intensity that comes from a great adventure. This is even more so after a long solo journey. All the little things that are normally overlooked in daily life are noticed as if for the first time, and communicating with people on a regular basis again is very draining.

On the evening of our arrival in Natimuk we had a few close friends over for drinks, as was our custom. Nothing big, nothing loud, a simple yarn in which the recently completed journey is hardly mentioned at all. This is good grounding for a person who has physically returned, but whose mind and spirit are still lost somewhere 'out there'.

Several days after returning home I drove the 300 kilometres to Melbourne to appear on the television chat show *The Panel*. Brigitte thought I should shave my beard, brush my hair and wear neat, clean clothes. I felt I should go as I was – dirty and dishevelled. The compromise we reached was perhaps inevitable – I shaved half my beard off, brushed one side of my hair, and pinned a dirty and torn shirt sleeve over my clean shirt.

The only reason I'd agreed to appear on the show was that in doing so I might help others – help inspire them, help motivate them. To show our youth that one can be 'successful' without conforming strictly to social conventions, without, for example, having completed high school let alone gone to university. By being comfortable in your individuality. Nevertheless, on a personal level, at that time it was the last thing I felt like doing. So when one of the regular panelists wanted to know if I ever asked myself 'Why am I doing this? Why am I doing this?', I answered in all honestly, 'Yes, as I drove down here to sit in front of these bright lights and cameras and three million people, it's a question I've been asking myself all day!'

After the show I drove to Eric Philips' home in Brighton to discuss the North Pole expedition, then just four-and-a-half months away. The prospect of having two huge expeditions in less than twelve months was tremendously exciting, and although I would not have wished for that particular timing, that's the way it was and there was never any question in my mind – I had to go. Eric is Australia's most widely experienced polar adventurer and the preparations for the expedition were well underway. Together we looked over maps and equipment, talking excitedly like a couple of schoolboys planning a weekend camp.

Driving home to Hope the following day felt like I was really going home. On arrival, after driving the winding tree-lined dirt road to the gate, I stepped out of the car and kissed the ground. Home felt secure, safe, a peaceful haven in which my body could recover from the massive ordeal that I had put it through. The familiarity of the mountains and their cliff lines grounded me.

The months that followed were relaxed and full of joy and contentment. I planted lots of vegetables, tended my garden and went hunting. Working together on the Great Mission had helped bring Brigitte and I closer than we had been in a number of years, and we luxuriated in the warmth of a deep love.

My strength slowly returned as the weeks and months passed and all too soon our departure date for the North Pole arrived. Part of me wished the trip was the following year, but we must seize the day or live in regret. I was going to the Arctic – it was my destiny, and to shy away from it was not in my nature.

We left Australia on 22 February 2002, and travelled to Siberia via Vienna and Moscow. We spent several days in the town of Khatanga, still very much in the grips of winter, before being flown to our start point off the islands of Severnaya Zemlya. Immediately after the helicopter departed we began, each of us hauling 140 kilograms of food and equipment behind us in plastic kayaks.

The Arctic is an ocean whose surface is a thin skin of frozen seawater. Tides, ocean currents and the wind continually move the ice causing it to fracture, which exposes the water below. The numerous plates of ice also slam into each other forcing ice up into pressure ridges of broken blocks up to 18 metres high. Across this extreme frozen icescape we marched for 1000 kilometres.

Right from the beginning I realised my recovery from the Great Mission had not been complete. I felt myself to be running at about 75 to 80 per cent of my optimal energy levels, and sorely missed the power I was lacking.

Fortunately I had the ultimate partner in Eric. With his awesome strength, stamina, resolve and motivation, it would have taken something extraordinary to stop us.

Our communications broke down, I fell in the ocean, we were harassed by a polar bear, some of our equipment failed, we suffered minor frostbite and we had our share of extreme weather, but after a gruelling 58 days we arrived triumphant at the North Pole. As the only successful team out of five from Siberia that year, we were immensely proud of our achievement, but most importantly we emerged from our ordeal with our friendship intact.

A more difficult challenge awaited me when I returned to an empty home. The love and passion Brigitte and I had shared had vanished, and so began another solo journey to the innermost corners of my soul. By isolating myself in the natural world, surrounded by my home at Hope, I was able to eliminate distractions and see my life with greater clarity. The past, present and future. My hopes and dreams. The power of my love.

Time and solitude, along with nature, enabled me to pass through that cold winter and emerge in the spring a new man. The love that pulses through my entire being remains, and my love has always been just that – mine. I see the future as a world filled with exciting potential which makes my spirit soar. Dreams that have previously seemed unattainable are now within reach and it is with a renewed sense of optimism that I look forward to their realisation.

Often now, some time since the mission, my mind wanders vividly back to those months alone with Seraphine, immersed within the slow pulsing rhythm of our ancient land. I can still feel the exultation of being one with all I encountered in that vast open space, and I long to return to the place where my heart and the land are joined.

LOG OF THE JOURNEY

- All distances are measured in kilometres, temperatures in degrees Celsius, and the water in litres.
- Distances logged do not include side trips in search of water, or back-tracking (e.g. when Jon went back 35 kilometres in search of his sleeping bag).
- Jon's original log included more information than presented below, omitted here for reasons of space.

Day	Date	Place	Distance over ground	Total distance over ground	Distance as crow flies	Total as crow flies	Hours marched (hrs, mins)	Estimated temp.	Water consumed
1	16/5	Mystery Island	1	1	1	1			
2	17/5	Mystery Island	0	1	0				
3	18/5	Mystery Island	0	1	0				
4	19/5	Mystery Island	0	1	0				
5	20/5	just S Nacoona Hill	15	16	12.5		4	23	3.8
6	21/5	nowhere	15	31	12		4	25	3.6
7	22/5	nowhere	15	46	12		4	25	4.1
8	23/5	nowhere	16	60	12	49.5	4	22	3.9
9	24/5	Willochra Creek	15	75	11	60.5	4, 50	23	3.8
10	25/5	near Poison Bore	15	90	10	70.5	4, 50	20	3.9
11	26/5	near Poison Bore	0	90	0	70.5	0	16	rain
12	27/5	Torrens	17	107	6	76.5	4, 50	16	4.0
13	28/5	Torrens	20	127	15	91.5	6, 10	17	4.1

14	29/5	Torrens, Etowie Creek	21	148	15.5	107	6	21	4.2
15	30/5	Torrens	20	168	15	122	6, 10	22	4
16	31/5	Torrens	22	190	16	138	6	20	4.1
17	1/6	Torrens	21	211	16.5	154.5	6, 10	18	4.2
18	2/6	Torrens, Nilpena Creek	20	231	14	168.5	6	23	4.6
19	3/6	Torrens, Warrioota Creek	23	254	15	183.5	7, 5	23	4.3
20	4/6	Torrens	11	265	8	191.5	3	22	4.5
21	5/6	Torrens, Nankabunyana Creek	21	286	16.5	208	6, 10	17	4.6
22	6/6	Torrens, Nankabunyana Creek	0	286	0	208	0	14	rain
23	7/6	Torrens, Depot Creek	16	302	13	221	6	17	puddles
24	8/6	Torrens	23	325	12	233	6, 10	18	3.8
25	9/6	Torrens	24	349	17	250	7	21	3.9
26	10/6	Torrens	24	373	17	267	7	18	3.8
27	11/6	Torrens	0	373	0	267	0	15	rain
28	12/6	Torrens	0	373	0	267	0	15	rain
29	13/6	Torrens	0	373	0	267	0	16	rain
30	14/6	Torrens, Salt Creek	27	400	20	287	7, 30	18	puddles
31	15/6	Flagstaff Lake	26	426	14	301	7	20	puddles
32	16/6	plateau ridge	24	450	14	315	7, 30	20	puddles
33	17/6	Clark Creek	28.5	478.5	20.5	335.5	7, 30	20	puddles
34	18/6	near Oodnadatta Track	26.5	505	20	355.5	7, 30	19	puddles

Day	Date	Place	Distance over ground	Total distance over ground	Distance as crow flies	Total as crow flies	Hours marched (hrs, mins)	Estimated temp.	Water consumed
35	19/6	Morris Creek	25	530	19	374.5	7, 30	20	puddles
36	20/6	near 2 mile tank	23	553	19	393.5	7, 30	20	puddles
37	21/6	Muloorina, Frome River	27	580	23	416.5	8	22	puddles
38	22/6	Muloorina, Frome River	0	580	0	416.5	0	22	river
39	23/6	Muloorina, Frome River	0	580	0	416.5	0	19	river
40	24/6	Lake Eyre	25	605	20	436.5	7	20	puddles
41	25/6	Tirari	24	629	19	457.5	8	23	puddles
42	26/6	Tirari	27	656	24.5	482	7, 45	22	puddles
43	27/6	Tirari, Cooper Creek	21	677	18	500	7, 30	20	puddles
44	28/6	Tirari, Lake Puntawolona	27	704	14	514	7, 30	18	puddles
45	29/6	Tirari, Lake Jeanine	27.5	731.5	23.5	537.5	8	19	puddles
46	30/6	Tirari, Lake Kalamurra	29	760.5	24.5	562	6, 30 day 1, 30 night	24	puddles in camel prints
47	1/7	Warburton, Wadlarkaninna	21	781.5	15	577	?	24	river
48	2/7	Warburton, Wadlarkaninna	0	781.5	0	577	0	24	river
49	3/7	Stony crossing meeting B	0	781.5	0	577	0	22	river
50	4/7	Warburton, Wadlarkaninna	0		0		0	18	river
51	5/7	Warburton, Wadlarkaninna	0		0		0	18	river

52	6/7	Warburton, Wadlarkaninna	0	781.5	0	577	0	18	river
53	7/7	Warburton	24	805.5	20	597	6	19	puddles
54	8/7	Warburton	34	839.5	29	626	8, 30	17	puddles
55	9/7	Warburton	33	872.5	27	653	7, 30	20	river
56	10/7	Warburton	25.5	898	22.5	675.5	7, 45	14	17.3
57	11/7	Warburton	0	898	0	675.5	0	14	rain
58	12/7	Warburton	0	898	0	675.5	0	17	river
59	13/7	Warburton near Rig Road	22	920	16.5	692	8, 30	19	river
60	14/7	Warburton, W bank	3	923	2.5	694.2	1	23	river
61	15/7	Warburton, W bank	250m	923	200m	694.2	0	10	rain
62	16/7	Warburton, W bank	0	923	0	694.2	0	15	rain
63	17/7	S edge Arunta	17	940	14	708.2	6	13	rain
64	18/7	S edge Arunta	20	960	15	723.2	7, 30	15	rain
65	19/7	S edge Arunta	21	981	16.5	739.7	8	16	river
66	20/7	Tepaminkanie Waterhole	15	996	11.5	751.7	8	18	river
67	21/7	Tepaminkanie Waterhole	0	996	0	751.7	0	20	river
68	22/7	nowhere	17	1013	10	761.7	9	20	river
69	23/7	Burt Waterhole	18	1031	10	771.7	8	22	river
70	24/7	Burt Waterhole	0	1031	0	771.7	0	22	river
71	25/7	Burt Waterhole	0	1031	0	771.7	0	22	river
72	26/7	Karrachie Waterhole	21	1052	16.5	788.2	6	20	river

Day	Date	Place	Distance over ground	Total distance over ground	Distance as crow flies	Total as crow flies	Hours marched (hrs, mins)	Estimated temp.	Water consumed
73	27/7	somewhere	25	1077	20	808.2	7, 30	20	river
74	28/7	Alton Downs	24	1101	19.5	827.7	8	21	river
75	29/7	Eyre Creek	27	1128	23.5	851.2	8	24	river
76	30/7	Ruwolts Bore	32	1160	29	880.2	8	24	river
77	31/7	Arunta	22	1182	18	898.2	7	25	river
78	1/8	Annandale Ruins (Creek)	21	1203	18	916.2	6	25	river
79	2/8	Muncoonie lakes	22	1225	17.5	933.7	7	24	river
80	3/8	Channel N of Muncoonie	25	1250	15.5	949.2	8	22	river
81	4/8	Kalidawarry Ruins (Mulligan)	24	1274	19.5	968.7	7, 30	25	river
82	5/8	Mulligan	27	1301	20.3	989.0	7, 30	21	river
83	6/8	Mulligan	23	1324	18	1007	7	20	river
84	7/8	Mulligan	27	1351	21.5	1028.5	8, 30	22	river
85	8/8	Mulligan, Teriwa Waterhole	28	1379	21.5	1049.5	8	21	river
86	9/8	Mulligan, Tiribilkie Waterhole	26	1405	22	1071.5	7, 30	23	river
87	10/8	Mulligan, Bindiacca Waterhole	25	1430	17.5	1089	8	24	river
88	11/8	Mulligan	26	1456	23	1112	8	21	river
89	12/8	Mulligan, Cootadoo Waterhole	22	1478	17.5	1129.5	6	24	river
90	13/8	nowhere	30	1508	26.5	1156	7, 30	20	river

91	14/8	nowhere	25	1533	22	1178	8	24	river
92	15/8	Lake Idamea, Pituri Creek	30	1563	26	1204	8	23	river
93	16/8	Georgina, Rabbit Waterhole	20	1583	15	1219	5	26	river
94	17/8	Georgina, Yanko Waterhole	23	1606	19	1238	7	21	river
95	18/8	Georgina just N of Roxborough access track	24	1630	20	1258	6		river
96	19/8	Georgina somewhere	25	1650	25	1283	7	22	river
97	20/8	Georgina somewhere	Return to search for sleeping bag					23	river
98	21/8	Georgina somewhere	Return to camp of Day 96					20	river
99	22/8	Georgina, Waukaba Waterhole	20	1670	15	1298	6	18	river
100	23/8	Georgina	17	1687	13	1311	4	20	river
101	24/8	Georgina, Mungala Waterhole	22	1709	17	1328	5, 30	20	river
102	25/8	Georgina somewhere	26	1735	22	1350	7	20	river
103	26/8	Georgina, just N of Urandangi	29	1764	26	1376	8	20	river
104	27/8	Georgina	35	1799	30	1406	9	18	river
105	28/8	Georgina	28	1827	23	1429	7, 30	18	river
106	29/8	Georgina	29	1856	24	1453	8	2	river
107	30/8	Georgina, Lake Nash Waterhole	19	1875	15	1468	4, 30	22	river
108	31/8	Georgina, un-named waterhole	18	1893	14	1482	5	18	river
109	1/9	Georgina, N end 8 Mile Waterhole	28	1919	22	1504	7	21	river
110	2/9	Georgina	26	1945	18.5	1522.5	8	24	river

Day	Date	Place	Distance over ground	Total distance over ground	Distance as crow flies	Total as crow flies	Hours marched (hrs, mins)	Estimated temp.	Water consumed
111	3/9	Georgina, Monkey Point Waterhole	25	1970	20.5	1543	7	25	river
112	4/9	Georgina near border	42	2012	34	1577	16	26	river
113	5/9	river	19	2031	16	1593	5	24	river
114	6/9	Chester Creek, Bullring Waterhole	29	2060	24	1617	8, 30	26	river
115	7/9	B. Bore, Morstone	30	2090	24	1641	8, 30	30	river
116	8/9	O'Shanassy tributary	29	2119	24	1665	7, 30	30	river
117	9/9	O'Shanassy River	23	2142	15	1680	6	28	river
118	10/9	O'Shanassy, just N of Thornton	27	2169	20	1700	9	26	river
119	11/9	O'Shanassy	23	2192	15	1715	7, 30	29	river
120	12/9	O'Shanassy	22	2214	17	1737	7	30	river
121	13/9	Gregory River, W bank	24	2238	11	1748	7	31	river
122	14/9	Gregory, near 175m summit	29	2267	23	1771	8	27	river
123	15/9	Gregory	30	2297	25	1796	8	26	river
124	16/9	Gregory, N of Gregory Downs	28	2325	24	1820	8	30	river
125	17/9	Gregory	35	2360	29	1849	9, 30	28	river
126	18/9	Gregory at Riverbend	34	2394	27	1876	9, 30	27	river
127	19/9	ford	42	2436	33	1899	10	26	river
128	20/9	Burketown	20	2456	20	1919	4	26	river

EQUIPMENT & FOOD LISTS

HAULING	kg
Arid Zone Cruiser (wheeled cart)	19.000
Hauling harness and chest bag	1.430
Leki ski poles	0.700
Bicycle pump	0.240
Inner-tube repair kit	0.210
2 × lightweight spanners	0.200
Total	**21.780**

NAVIGATION

Maps, original 1/250,000	1.060
Maps, photocopies	0.380
Map case	0.120
Spherical compass	0.110
2 × Silva compasses	0.260
2 × watches	0.175
Total	**2.105**

CAMPING

Tarpaulin	1.820
Mosquito net	0.410
2 × sleeping bags	2.100
Ridgerest sleeping mat	0.460
Head torch	0.160
1 bowl	0.060
8-litre alloy pot	0.520
Toothbrush and paste	0.110
Total	**5.640**

CLOTHING

Fairydown lightweight Gortex Jacket	0.660
Fairydown lightweight Gortex pants	0.400
Silk inner sheet	0.200
Neoprene knee warmers	0.280
Hat	0.340
Fly net	0.060
Sun-protection gloves	0.040
Woollen fingerless gloves	0.040
Sun-protection scarf	0.060
2 × cotton shirts	0.740
2 × cotton pants	0.930
1 pair thick socks	0.150
6 pairs thin socks	0.330
4 pairs underwear	0.310
Gaiters	0.400
Fairydown lightweight down jacket	0.680
Thermal balaclava	0.040
1 light woollen jumper	0.440
Thongs	0.300
Boots	1.850
Total	**8.250**

WATER

1 × 20-litre water container	0.900
2 × 20-litre collapsible water containers	0.840
2 × 10-litre wine bladders	0.260
3 × 3-litre water bottles	0.400

1 × 1-litre water bottle	0.080
Distillation plant	3.120
Total	**5.600**

FOOD

Rice	8.000
Flour	8.000
Muesli	6.000
80 × Freedom Food bars	8.000
Assorted chocolate bars	2.000
22 × freeze-dried meals	2.350
Olive oil	2.000
Ensure	2.000
Peanut butter	0.500
Honey	0.500
Promite	0.250
Miso	0.250
4 loaves home-baked bread	3.400
Potatoes	1.000
Tomatoes	1.000
Salami	0.500
15 × Fisherman's Friend	0.375
Total	**46.125**

HUNTING/GATHERING

General-purpose knife	0.200
Skinning knife	0.140
Diamond sharpener and stone	0.120
Plastic digging trowel	0.060
3 × large cotton scarves	0.160
.303 Rifle	3.840
.22 Rifle	1.900
140 rounds ammunition	0.860
Total	**7.280**

FILMING

Video

Solar panel	0.690
Sony PD100 video camera	1.100
Solar power connector	0.100
Video stock	1.580
3 × batteries	0.760
Microphone and extension	0.400
Wide-angle lens	0.400
Head cleaner	0.080
Blower brush and tissue	0.010
Tripod	1.220
Case	1.250
Manuals	0.340

Still

Olympus mju	0.230
Minolta SLR 19mm–35mm lens	1.120
Film stock	0.930
Total	**10.210**

SERAPHINE'S FOOD AND EQUIPMENT

First aid	0.270
Dry dog biscuits	6.000
Dried meat	0.500
Water bowl	0.040
Eating bowl	0.040
Fur coat	0.190
Fleece-lined raincoat	0.160
boots	0.048
Total	**7.248**

MISCELLANEOUS

2 pairs Bolle sunglasses	0.130
Leatherman	0.275
Repair kit	1.040
3 rolls toilet paper	0.460
Suncream and zinc	0.250
Journal	0.500
Bush food notes	0.650
2 books	0.800
Extra cord and bungee	0.800
Baby karabiners	0.200
Kitbags and stuff sacks	2.100
EPIRB (emergency beacon)	0.250
First aid kit	1.040
Total	**8.495**
Grand total	**122.733**

BUSH TUCKER GATHERED/HUNTED

Plants
- Acacia gum
- Bulrush
- Bush banana
- Conkerberry
- Desert bloodwood galls
- Desert quandong
- Devils twine
- Fig
  - – cluster
  - – rock
  - – sandpaper
- Golden grevillea

Manna and Lerp
Mistletoes
Nardoo
Native lasiandra
Native pear
New Zealand spinach
Nitre bush
Parakeelya
Pepper-cress
Pigweed
Ruby saltbush
Saltbush
Samphire
Sandalwood fruit
Sawthistle
Sea purslane
Tar vine
Ulcardo melon
Water lily

Meat
- Bloated bovine
- Bloodwood gall grub
- Cat
- Duck
- Fish
- Freshwater mussel
- Grasshopper
- Kangaroo
- Lizard
- Pig
- Rabbit
- Snake
- Termite
- Witchetty grub